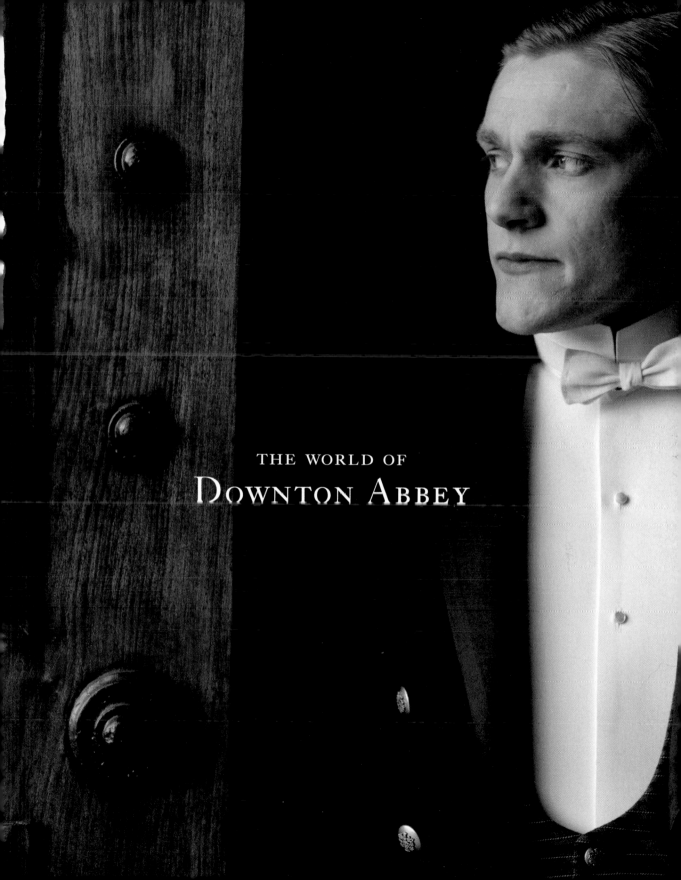

THE WORLD OF
DOWNTON ABBEY

Dear Mr. Crawley,

Forgive me writing but you
may have heard that our cousins,
James and Patrick Crawley,
were drowned when the Titanic
foundered. You may also be
aware that, in consequence you
are heir presumptive to the
titles.

Lady Grantham and
I to your attention and
wish to invite you down so that
you may know us
which

A CARNIVAL FILMS / MASTERPIECE CO-PRODUCTION

THE WORLD OF
DOWNTON ABBEY

TEXT
JESSICA FELLOWES

PHOTOGRAPIIY
NICK BRIGGS

FOREWORD
JULIAN FELLOWES

ST. MARTIN'S PRESS
NEW YORK

LORD GRANTHAM

*'My dear fellow. We all have chapters
we would rather keep unpublished.'*

Contents

Foreword

I have always enjoyed country houses. There is something about their completeness, with their different rooms and offices catering to almost every need, making up a microcosm of a complete world, that is very satisfactory to me. But, as a child, wandering around the homes of my parents' friends and relations, I was aware that I was looking at the remains of a way of life that, with rare exceptions, was no longer being lived in by them. Those empty attic rooms, often still boasting an iron bedstead or a dusty cupboard with vacant nameplate holders on the doors, spoke of a once-crowded place, peopled then only by ghosts. Those echoing stables, full of abandoned toys and rusting gardening equipment, those vast kitchens, jammed with discarded luggage and broken bicycles and signs for use in the village fête, were haunted to my childish eyes by shadows of what used to be.

Of course, I grew up in the sad years for these monuments to the past. They had lost their value as the aristocracy largely threw in the towel after the war, and in the 1950s they could hardly be given as presents. Instead, palace after great palace, those that were not considered suitable for some new and frequently inappropriate role, fell victim to the demolition ball, and an immense part of our nation's heritage was literally thrown away. Until 1974, when the new director of the Victoria and Albert Museum, Roy Strong, decided to stage an exhibition, *The Destruction of the English Country House*, and it is not an exaggeration to say that everything changed, almost overnight. We woke up to the idea that these houses were an integral part of our history, that the life formerly lived in them had involved us all, whether our forebears had been behind the green baize door or in front of it, that they were not simply huge and unmanageable barns, no longer viable without sufficient staff, but expressions of our national character that we should be proud of.

And as we learned to love them again, so a younger generation invented a new way to live in them. They didn't mourn the servants they had usually never known. They simply saw the space and its possibilities. The big kitchens were re-opened and the horrible converted ante-rooms and passages that had served as kitchens for our parents' generation were abandoned. But this time, the family chose to occupy the kitchens in their own way, importing televisions and sofas and toys and making them right for the way we live now. Helpers did not sleep upstairs in the garrets but came in from the village and called the owners by their Christian names and felt, quite rightly, that they had a stake in making the house work. In a way, the landowners reinvented themselves, as the aristocracy has done so many times before, and found a place, for themselves and their houses, in modern Britain. This was perhaps the main inspiration for the series, *Downton Abbey*, because we did all feel that were we to go into this territory, it must be right for our present *zeitgeist* to give equal weight, in terms of narrative or moral probity or even likeability to both parts of the community of a great house, the family and their servants. This I hope we have done, favouring neither group over the other, which I am convinced remains one of the principal strengths of the show.

Like most of the good things in my life, *Downton Abbey* came about entirely by chance. I had been trying to get a completely different project off the ground with the producer, Gareth Neame, and when at last we realised it was not going to fly, we met for dinner to call it a day. It was then that Gareth suggested venturing back into the territory of a film I had written some years before, *Gosford Park*, but this time for television, and that is how it began. *Gosford* was set in a large country house in November 1932 and it dealt with a shooting party and their servants, both those working in the house and for the guests, so it was clear at once what Gareth wanted. I was a little nervous initially, at the risks of asking for a second helping, but the idea grew on me and so *Downton Abbey* was born. Television – or rather, a television series, with its open-endedness, with its unlimited time to develop any character – held possibilities that the space allowed for a film narrative could not offer. We decided at once to retreat twenty years to 1912, since the underlying theme of *Gosford Park* had been that it was all coming to an end; but we didn't want to go further back than that as we both agreed that we needed the action to take place in a recognisable universe – with cars and trains and telephones and many other modern devices, albeit in embryo, which defined the period clearly as the parent of the present day.

As to why I find the subject so appealing, I suppose it is because that half century from around 1890 to 1940 seems to me to form a bridge from the old world into the new. At the beginning, society was run along much the same lines it had been since the Conquest. Inventions had altered things, of course, but the strict pyramid shape, the idea that everyone had their different roles to play and that, to a great extent, they were born to play them, was still unchallenged, or so it appeared. In fact, of course, beneath the smooth surface of the long Edwardian summer, a good deal was being questioned. Trades unions, women's rights, Marxism, were all waiting in the wings and it would only take a couple of years of war before they started to stride centre stage. New modes of travel would shrink the world, new methods of production would transform it. For most of the population of Monarchical Old Europe, at least for those who were young adults at the turn of the last century, the world they would die in would bear almost no resemblance to the world of their beginnings, whatever their nationality, whatever their class.

My own great-aunt Isie, the model for Violet Grantham, was born in 1880, making her more than ten years older than Lady Mary Crawley, and she would die at ninety one in 1971, so I knew her well. She was one of the generation of young ladies who never went to school and her Mama would only allow her to attend university lectures in London if she agreed to two conditions: the first that she would never sit an exam, the second that she would be accompanied at all times by a maid. She was presented in 1898, married before the First World War and set up house in one of the Cadogans, 'quite near Peter Jones, dear,' with a butler who had been first footman to Mrs Willie James, reputedly the illegitimate daughter of King Edward VII. She lost her husband in the first war, her only son in the second, and she would live to see men land on the moon. From knowing her and listening to her story, a clear sense came to me that 'history' is not so long ago.

For most of them, the way of life lived at Downton would come to an end in 1939. Of course there would be people after the war who employed butlers and cooks, there are quite a few of them now, but as a way of life lived, to a degree, in every village and hamlet from Land's End to John o'Groats, it was over. Many of the houses were requisitioned by the services, some to their cost, and the debts and mortgages accumulated since the collapse of the agricultural economy in the 1880s and 90s, made the idea of re-opening them when the fighting ended six years later, unalluring. Their renaissance would not come for thirty years or so after the Second World War and then, as I have said, the new owners chose to live in them differently. Happily, this revival has, in many cases, proved successful and Britain's old families have written and continue to write another chapter in their long history. Which brings us back to the Crawleys of Downton Abbey, but when it comes to how far we will travel with them through the decades of challenge and change that lie ahead for their civilisation, that must remain to be seen.

Julian Fellowes
July 2011

Family Life

CHAPTER ONE

CHARLES CARSON
Butler

ELSIE HUGHES
Housekeeper

JOHN BATES
Lord Grantham's Valet

SARAH O'BRIEN
Lady Grantham's Lady's Maid

BERYL PATMORE
Cook

ANNA SMITH
Head Housemaid

GWEN DAWSON
Housemaid

ETHEL PARKS
Housemaid

DAISY ROBINSON
Kitchen Maid

THOMAS BARROW
First Footman

WILLIAM MASON
Second Footman

TOM BRANSON
Chauffeur

VIOLET
THE DOWAGER COUNTESS
OF GRANTHAM

ROBERT
THE EARL
OF GRANTHAM

CORA
THE COUNTESS
OF GRANTHAM

LADY MARY
CRAWLEY

LADY EDITH
CRAWLEY

LADY SYBIL
CRAWLEY

ISOBEL CRAWLEY

MATTHEW CRAWLEY

April 1912.
The sun is rising behind Downton Abbey, a great and
splendid house in a great and splendid park. So secure
does it appear that it seems as if the way of life it
represents will last for another thousand years.

It won't.

*W*elcome to the world of Downton Abbey, a place that has captivated an audience of millions, all following the lives of one family and their servants. Against the backdrop of a fading Edwardian society, we watch their personal dramas unfold and see them through the horrors and change that the First World War brought to Britain. This perhaps is what fascinates us: not just the beautiful scenery, the sumptuous costumes, nor even the skill of the actors, but the fact that we are experiencing something of how life was a hundred years ago. We notice the differences between our lives and theirs; the rigid social hierarchy, the nuances of etiquette, the stifling clothes and the battle for women to be heard. But alongside this, we see something that is the same: family life.

At the forefront of everything at Downton is *family*, whether this stands for the blood ties of the Crawleys or the relationships between the servants below stairs. All of us can recognise a familiar character amongst them: Violet, the dowager Countess, the old-fashioned grandmother; Mary, Edith and Sybil, the squabbling sisters; Robert and Cora, the loving parents; or Rosamund, the interfering sister-in-law. Any of us who have left behind our families to make our own new, adopted ties with those we work with or with friends we choose are creating a new family, just as the servants do at Downton. With Carson and Mrs Hughes as the firm but fair parents, Thomas and O'Brien as the scheming siblings and Daisy as the baby, the servants are close by on the other side of the green baize door that separates upstairs and downstairs. Thrown together in cramped quarters, working long, hard hours, the servants nevertheless find security in

Hugh Bonneville is Lord Grantham

'Downton Abbey is a microcosm of society. It had its own machinery that needed to keep working – it's not masters and slaves but had its own order in which everyone depended on each other to keep it going.'

Dan Stevens is Matthew

'There's no such thing as a typical day's filming, but if it's a full
day, I'll be collected by car at 5.30am and driven to Highclere
to meet other bleary-eyed actors. After breakfast and 20
minutes in the make-up chair, I'm ready to start shooting.
Sometimes we manage two or three scenes in a morning, but
often it takes that long for a single scene. Lunch is a good
chance to sit on the bus and chat to the other actors and crew.
We shoot more scenes in the afternoon until tea and cake at
4pm, which causes a flurry. We can't take any food or drink
that's not water into the house, so we usually cower under a
rain shelter, but if there's glorious sunshine we can have tea on
the lawn. We wrap about 7pm and then I'm driven home.'

their relationships with each other. Like all families, they have their ups and their downs, their favourites and a few petty fights.

Downton Abbey is more than just a house, it is also a home to both the family and the servants. Everyone living here is striving to keep the house and estate in good order, ready to pass on to the next generation. So when the question is raised of who will inherit, everyone is affected – above and below stairs. Even a miniature kingdom needs to know who is king.

For the moment, of course, Robert, the Earl of Grantham, is still the master of his realm. In this role, he has his own duties to fulfil just as much as Daisy, the scullery maid at the very bottom of the pecking order. A place like Downton Abbey cannot run well unless everyone within it understands their role and carries out their work efficiently.

There is a clear hierarchy at Downton; each servant has a position. The maids deal with the laundry, but the finishing of the clothes for the master and mistress of the house is the responsibility of Bates, valet to Lord Grantham, and Miss O'Brien, lady's maid to Lady Grantham. These servants enjoy senior roles in the household, are two of the few that move seamlessly between below stairs and above, and enjoy the confidence of their employers. The rest of the staff probably think that these two have easier daily routines than the other servants, having nothing more to attend to than the earl and his wife's needs. But from the first cup of tea brought up in the morning to whatever they might want last thing at night, they must be on duty all day with little respite. Their relationship with their employers is one of trust and practicality: Bates and O'Brien are welcome in the bedrooms, dressing rooms and even the bathrooms of their employers, making them privy to many details of the family's private lives, and giving them a powerful position in the household. They could use this to their advantage when back downstairs, teasing or threatening the other staff with it – as when O'Brien learns before anyone else that the heir to Downton Abbey has been drowned during the *Titanic* disaster.

By contrast, the housemaids – Anna, Ethel, Gwen and Daisy – work behind the scenes. They are up early to complete the dusting of the drawing room and libraries, the plumping of the cushions, the cleaning of the grates and the laying of the fires before the family comes downstairs for breakfast. Only when the bedrooms are empty do the maids go in, to change the sheets and refresh the biscuit jars and water carafes. The rest of the day is spent on cleaning tasks set by the housekeeper, Mrs Hughes, such as beating rugs or polishing brass, as well as assisting the daughters of

A DAY IN THE LIFE OF DAISY

4.30am: In the small, dark hours of the morning, the kitchen maid, Daisy, awakes alone, dresses herself in her hand-me-down corset, simple dress and apron and steals down the stairs to stoke the kitchen fire. She creeps round the family's bedrooms to light their fires, before going down to the kitchen to blacken the stove and lay the breakfast things in the servants' hall.

6am: Daisy knocks on the doors of the housemaids to waken them, then takes her basket of logs with brushes, blacking, matches and paper to lay and light the fires in the rooms on the ground floor – the libraries, drawing room, dining room and great hall. The hall boy, another lowly servant who was only occasionally seen and never heard, has already delivered the coal and kindling wood to the scuttles.

10am: Daisy is still in suds up to her elbows as William and Thomas bring the cleared breakfast things, except for the glasses, which they wash in the servery. There's no respite even as the last plate is stacked to dry; Mrs Patmore tells her to start on scrubbing pots and pans needed for lunch before she chops vegetables.

2pm: Once luncheon has been served and cleared away, Daisy has to wash all the pans and crockery once more, ready for dinner.

4pm: The servants enjoy tea, although not all of them can sit down at the same time. This well-earned break ends with the dressing gong, which marks the time when the family retires upstairs to dress for dinner.

7pm: By now, Daisy has been up for 13 hours but she cannot allow her eyelids to droop. The busiest part of her day is about to begin with the final preparations for the family supper, as well as laying out the servants' supper.

8.30pm: The pots and pans, which had been scoured to gleaming after luncheon, ready for cooking dinner, need to be cleaned again now that it has been served.

9.45pm: When the family's dinner is finished, Daisy puts her aching hands into the hot soapy water for the last time that day, cleaning the crockery and cutlery. Once she has had something to eat herself in the kitchen, the cook will send her to bed, much to her chagrin – it's only when the servants have finished their work for the day and are relaxing in the servants' hall after dinner that the fun begins.

Tomorrow will be the same again. With just one half day off a week, the routine is relentless. At the end of her arduous day, Daisy trudges wearily up the stairs to her room. Just a few hours later, she'll wake again to another day in Downton Abbey.

Writer, Julian Fellowes

'In a house this size, there would normally be a scullery maid, who did the washing up; a vegetable maid, who prepared the vegetables; and a stillroom maid who did the baking. For the purposes of narration, we amalgamated several maids' jobs into one for Daisy.'

Writer, Julian Fellowes

'While bells are now seen as a symbol of servitude, at the time the bell-boards came in, around the 1820s, they were hailed as an absolute liberation. Up until that point, the footmen had to sit on hard wooden chairs within earshot of the family – usually in the hall. They would get a message, say, "Please ask my maid to come and see me", then have to go downstairs, find the maid and then go back to their chair. With the bell-board, they could not only simply be wherever they wanted to be but if the bell rang from, say, the mistress's bedroom, it was immediately obvious who was needed.'

the house or any female guests who come to stay without their maids. They can be called upon at any time; each room in the house has a cord, pulled to summon assistance. The cord is connected to a wire that rings one of many bells on a board in the servants' hall below; each labelled with the relevant room so the appropriate servant can attend. The jangle of bells is a sound that rules the servants' lives.

THOMAS
'And they're off.'

Carson, the butler, is the most senior member of the below-stairs family, overseeing the work of all the male servants, and is Lord Grantham's right-hand man. Butlers were sometimes grand enough to attain a little notoriety: Edwin Lee, the long-serving butler for Cliveden, an estate comparable to Downton in size and splendour, was known even by guests as 'Lord Lee'. While the butler's practical duties are few – monitoring the wine cellar, decanting port, pouring wine at the dinner table, and cleaning the fine pieces of silver (the footmen clean the rest) – he is the one who makes sure that everything is running exactly as it should be, and woe betide the footman who neglects to snap to attention. Carson believes the responsibility for the entire house is his, and if there is no one to do something that needs doing, he'll do it himself. When they are short-handed during the war, he risks his own health rather than let standards slip.

Alongside Carson is Mrs Hughes, the housekeeper, who is in charge of the housemaids – both their work and their welfare. With a big bunch of keys jangling at her waist, she manages the household accounts, draws up the servants' rotas, checks the linens (sheets and tablecloths are used in rotation so they last for years) and keeps a careful eye on orders for the kitchen store cupboard. This last responsibility, of course, is a bone of contention between Mrs Hughes and the cook, Mrs Patmore, who cannot understand why the stores do not fall under her jurisdiction.

Working long hours in a kitchen that was boiling hot all year round, cooks were famously short-tempered, understandably so when you learn that Mrs Patmore is up before 6am and won't go to bed until 18 hours later, after cooking eight meals for the family and the servants.

Attending to guests

Gordon Grimmett was second footman at Cliveden while it was the country home of the Astors. The many high-profile guests, including film stars, politicians and writers such as Charlie Chaplin, Gandhi, T.E. Lawrence and Winston Churchill, meant a lot of work for the staff. 'Every morning would see us up at seven, running down to the stillroom, eventually emerging with six small morning tea trays arranged on one large butler's tray, distributing them round the guests' rooms, opening curtains and gently but firmly waking them. We didn't want them slipping back to sleep again and blaming us for their having missed breakfast. Then we collected their clothes from the night before, and whipped them into the brushing-room, to sponge, brush, fold and hang them. Then we would be laying up the breakfast table, and bringing in the various dishes ... and the constant running to and fro with fresh toast.'

PREPARING FOR HOUSE PARTIES

The arrival of guests at a house such as Downton is an important event not only for the family, but for the servants, too. Most household staff had real pride in their work and the house in which they served, and visits were a chance to show just how good they were at their jobs. The presence of a very noble visitor, such as a Duke, was considered an honour and the servants would be eager to serve him and make sure that he left feeling that their house was a well-run one.

CARSON

'It's certainly a great day for Downton, to welcome a Duke under our roof.'

Preparations at Downton are begun by Cora, who decides which bedrooms will be used, then the right menus are put together with Mrs Patmore – for meals that will show off the best of the home farm produce as well as the cook's ability to create a worthy feast. Once agreed, the menus are written in French. Cora then decides the placement around the dining table at each meal in advance. At the lunches and dinners, if more people are staying than the footmen could reasonably be expected to serve, the valet is asked to help. Carson might help out in the dining room if necessary, but never a maid – although this rule had to be relaxed on occasion during the war when there weren't enough men.

Mrs Hughes then makes sure the bedrooms are made up freshly on the day of the guests' arrival, and clean towels and new soaps are placed in the bathroom. Inkwells must be full, and sheets of Downton Abbey writing paper and envelopes must be laid out on the bedroom table. The head gardener is asked to supply cut flowers for the house and for an arrangement in a vase for each of the guests' bedrooms.

If the visitors arrive without either a valet or lady's maid of their own, a footman or housemaid is assigned to them. Branson, the chauffeur, is despatched to the station to meet everyone off the train. Arriving at the house, they are greeted by Lord and Lady Grantham and their daughters, Carson, and William and Thomas, who take the luggage.

Guest luggage is unpacked in a room that has a series of locker-like cupboards. If several ladies are staying, this is the opportunity for their maids to compare the dresses planned for the Saturday-to-Monday and thus avoid anyone wearing anything too similar at the same time.

The footmen, Thomas and William, are the servants most visible to the family and any guests, and therefore they are dressed in tailored livery. They answer the front door, deliver messages to the village, serve in the dining room and stoke the fire if a member of the family is in the room. William is also in charge of walking Pharaoh, Lord Grantham's Labrador, first thing in the morning and last thing at night, and Thomas has been given the unusual responsibility of cleaning all the clocks in the house, because his father was a clockmaker. Footmen were often known for their arrogance – their appearance gave them an advantage over the rest of the servants and they weren't afraid to use it.

MRS HUGHES

'You have to ease up a bit or you'll give yourself a heart attack. Things cannot be the same when there's a war on.'

CARSON

'I do not agree. Keeping up standards is the only way to show the Germans they will not beat us in the end.'

Below stairs, the day begins early, and breakfast is eaten after completing their morning tasks but before the family come down from their bedrooms. Gordon Grimmett, third footman at Longleat House during the First World War, did not look forward to breaking his fast in the morning: 'It was a picnic kind of meal with people coming and leaving as their duties required. There was little variety, it seemed it was always kedgeree on weekdays and bacon on Sundays. As it was war time we were each given a quarter of a pound of butter a week, which we kept in a small tin; once that was gone it was dry bread.'

Lord Grantham and his daughters, as well as any guests, arrive in the dining room for breakfast at around 9am – Lady Grantham is absent, as married women enjoy the privilege of breakfast in bed. The footmen serve tea, as well as coffee and hot toast, but otherwise everyone helps

Phyllis Logan is Mrs Hughes

'I like the scenes with Carson. In those moments they have
a chance to be themselves, because they've always got his
character very much in charge. Carson takes it all very seriously,
but when he has his little chats with Mrs Hughes that's his one
opportunity for a bit of a release. So I do enjoy those scenes.'

The kitchen staff worked the longest hours of all the servants, from the early morning start baking bread and preparing a cooked breakfast, until the servants' supper late at night, not to mention the washing up of pots, pans and crockery in between. In every large house, the kitchen was the workplace of the cook and her 'family', who discouraged the interference of other servants; neither the butler nor the housekeeper, nor indeed any of their staff, were welcome within it without a good reason.

Although hard on her staff in the heat and bustle of the day, Mrs Patmore has her moments as a caring matriarch of her kitchen family, dishing out advice to Daisy, as the youngest member of her staff. The division between the servants applies to meals, too, with Mrs Patmore and her kitchen staff always eating separately in their own dominion; there they can all finally put their feet up in an atmosphere that is less stuffy than that of the servants' hall, where the butler is on alert for any cheekiness and the housekeeper keeps a beady eye on any flirtation, poised to stamp it out with a fierce glare.

Apple Charlotte

2 lb Cooking apples
4 ozs of Brown Sugar
1 oz. Butter
1 Lemon
3 ozs. Granose flakes

Peel, Core and Slice the apples Place a layer on the bottom of a pie dish Sprinkle with Sugar, lemon rind and lemon juice and Cover with granose flakes. Repeat until the dish is full letting the granose flakes form the top layer. Cover with greased paper bake for 3/4 to 1 hour. then turn the dish and

Garden Party

Food
Cucumber Sandwiches.
Pompadour Sandwiches
Poched Salmon.
Parsley Potatoes
Game Terrine.

Carson   Refreshments.
- Wine.
- Champagne.   Lemonade
                        Elderflower Cordial
                        Ginger beer.

Sweets
Elderflower and fruit jelly
Scones served with cream
                   - Choice of preserves

Apple Tarts
Rhubarb fool with Almond biscuits

Lesley Nicol is Mrs Patmore

'The basis for everything is something the historical advisor said to me: "Consider this like a show. It's got to be the best show." Then I got it. When someone comes to stay, they've got to leave saying it was perfect. My character has enormous pride and commitment. It just can't go wrong, she can't allow things to go wrong. But what else has she got? That's her life.'

A typical menu for the family, in a house such as Downton Abbey,
might consist of the following:

First course
Watercress soup, Fillets of Turbot à la Crème,
Fried Filleted Soles and Anchovy Sauce

Entrées
Larded Fillets of Rabbits,
Tendrons de Veau with Purée of Tomatoes

Second course
Stewed Rump of Beef à la Jardinière,
Roast Fowl, Boiled Ham,
Roast Pigeons or Larks

Third course
Rhubarb Tartlets, Meringues,
Clear Jelly, Cream, Ice Pudding, Soufflé

Roquefort and Brie Cheese

themselves. This is the most informal meal of the day, when the family themselves lift the lids of silver chafing dishes, kept warm by small oil burners beneath and laden with bacon, eggs, devilled kidneys and porridge. Cold slices of tongue, ham and grouse are placed on the sideboard. Cornflakes, called 'Post Toasties', which have come from America, are on the table, with milk from the house's dairy.

Alongside the endless cooking, the cook has to supervise the preparation of everything that comes out of her kitchen. She has an army of kitchen maids to help her, as everything from consommé to horseradish sauce must be made from scratch, not to mention the constant baking – every loaf of bread, cake and biscuit is homemade, ready for elevenses as well as afternoon tea.

MRS PATMORE

'No! Listen to me! And take those kidneys up to the servery before I knock you down and serve your brains as fritters.'

Dinner is the big event for everyone in the house. Dressed in white tie, the family would assemble in the drawing room, where they would talk but not drink. In London there is a growing fashion for cocktails before dinner, but it hasn't reached Downton yet. At dinner, with three courses at the very least – five if there are important guests – Mrs Patmore does her best to show off her culinary finesse (for the family anyway; the servants make do with simpler fare such as lamb stew and semolina, prepared by the kitchen maids).

At the table, Lord Grantham sits in the middle on one side, his wife opposite, as the Royals do. His mother, Violet, sits at his right as the next grandest woman in the room. Carson pours the wine and Thomas and William, wearing gloves (only footmen wore gloves and only to wait at table – never for any other task), serve the food, à la Russe. They begin by serving whoever is sitting on Lord Grantham's right and work their way clockwise around the table, men and women alternately. The modern restaurant fashion for 'ladies first' is continental. The serving dish is held on

BEHIND THE GREEN BAIZE DOOR

From the early hours of the morning until late at night, the servants are permanently on duty to attend to all the demands of the house and family. Below stairs, just a few moments of calm may be snatched during the day and are a welcome relief indeed.

Once the family have finished breakfast and gone about their business for the day, everyone has a list of chores to get on with until lunch. There is a brief respite for the servants' midday meal at around noon before the machine is set in motion again for the family to be served their lunch promptly at 1pm. At about 4pm the servants are given bread and cheese by the cook and this must keep them going until they have their supper, a substantial two courses, but only after the family have finished theirs and the dining room has been cleared away. The crockery is brought downstairs for Daisy to wash up, but the glasses are left in the servery – they will be carefully cleaned the next day.

THOMAS

'This isn't her territory.
We can say what we like, down here.'

Supper for the servants is always looked forward to – their work is over and it is the longed-for moment when they can all breathe, kick back and relax. It is also a time when the staff can have time to themselves away from the family and can indulge in some gossip about the goings-on in the house and amongst their employers. As Alastair Bruce, historical advisor, told the actors: for the servants, observing the family upstairs was the equivalent of watching *Coronation Street* or *EastEnders* today. But although the atmosphere is informal at the end of their working hours, lapses of manners are not permitted. Carson ensures that the servants of the house continue to reflect the gentility of the people they serve. A strict order of precedence is set around the table, just as in the dining room upstairs. Mrs Hughes sits at the right hand of Carson, the footmen sit by the butler, the head housemaid and lady's maid by the housekeeper, with the lower-ranking servants at the other end of the table. In a house such as Downton Abbey, there is no concept of 'off-duty'.

Knowing your place

On set, there is a genuine sense of an above
and below-stairs division. On the first day
Alastair Bruce divided the cast into 'above'
and 'below' and they were put in different
rooms to hear his talk on what life would have
been like for them. Once they were filming,
many of the below-stairs cast worked nearly
all the time at Ealing Studios, rarely venturing
to the big house to film at Highclere Castle,
and vice versa. Lesley Nicol, who plays Mrs
Patmore, says: 'When you do a job like this,
you start to take on the genuine feelings of
your character. So when I went to Highclere, I
felt very small indeed! It was overwhelming to
be there.'

Siobhan Finneran is O'Brien

'I loved filming all the scenes round the
servants' hall table. We all get on very well
and there's such a good atmosphere there,
where you can get a bit lost at Highclere. I
think we probably drove the directors mad
because we're all so noisy, but I think that
helps the scenes.'

Elizabeth McGovern is Cora

'I think Cora is very much an emotionally connected mother. As an American she would have a distinctive approach, different to the English aristocracy's way of doing things. Her instinct is to be involved with the day-to-day and to go about things in a more hands-on way.'

the diner's left while they help themselves. Finished plates are collected from the right-hand side. Only when Lord Grantham has the decanter of port and glasses (he will pour it himself) in the dining room and the women have been served coffee in the drawing room, may the servants have their supper. It is their first chance to relax since they started their working day.

Away from the steaming hubbub that is the kitchen, the cogs of the estate turn at a rapid pace. Occasionally, the outside world intrudes. Deliveries are made throughout the day – newspapers early in the morning (*The Times* for his Lordship, *The Daily Sketch* for her Ladyship), fresh vegetables and meat from the home farm, produce from the dairy and goods from village shops. Post was delivered and collected twice a day – the family 'posted' their letters into a box in the hall, which had a sign on it: 'Post will be collected at 9am and 4pm'. The butler took these letters, stamped them and gave them to the postman. The system was efficient – if a letter was received in the morning, a reply sent in second post arrived the next day. Telegrams were sent and received within hours; the footmen were dispatched to the Post Office with any urgent message to be relayed.

While Lord Grantham does not have a paid job – hence the family's shock at Matthew Crawley's intention to carry on his work as a solicitor – he is kept busy with the affairs of the estate. He is helped by members of the extended servants' family: an estate manager who oversees the farm as well as the tenants' cottages, and a gamekeeper who rears and protects the game and their cover for the shooting season, not forgetting the head gardener and his team of several under-gardeners. There are grooms, too, for the horses used for riding, hunting and to draw carriages.

Lady Grantham does not concern herself with the business of running the estate, but she has plenty of matters of her own that need attention. As the châtelaine, she is important to anybody who wishes to use the influence of the house – a fund-raising effort or the village flower show, for example. She also works closely with Mrs Hughes to ensure that any guests are well looked after, deciding which room they are staying in and which maid or footman will see to their requirements during their visit, if needed. Placement cards for the dinner table must also be written. Lady Grantham would also decide who to put next to whom at dinner, strictly observing the precedence of rank, of course. Whether entertaining visitors or not, each morning she would consult with Mrs Patmore in Cora's sitting room for half an hour or so, and look over the day's menu.

LOOKING AFTER THE FAMILY

While there were daily jobs that required everyone to work together in a synchronised way, such as mealtimes, there were many other essential tasks and details that needed addressing which were allocated to specific servants.

Carson, as butler, ensures that every member of his staff is occupied before retreating to his pantry to carry out jobs such as paperwork and decanting port. The perfect port at dinner must be poured in front of a lit candle, to check the colour, into a funnel covered with gauze to catch any dregs. Julian Fellowes was taught this method by Arthur Inch, footman to the Londonderry family before the war, and the advisor on *Gosford Park*. A scene was filmed showing this, but it was later cut, so Julian was delighted to be able to use it in *Downton Abbey*.

DAISY

'Why are their papers ironed?'

O'BRIEN

'To dry the ink, silly. We wouldn't want his Lordship's hands to be as black as yours.'

Miss O'Brien is perhaps the most sophisticated of the servants; to perform her role she must be skilled in dressing hair and the art of a lady's toilette. She also has to be accomplished in fine sewing, as she is expected to mend her lady's dresses and make some of her undergarments. Similarly, Bates must ensure his Lordship's wardrobe is immaculate and ready to be worn whenever it is required, which means polishing cufflinks and shoes and mending any damaged garments. Servants learned the tricks of the trade by experience – their own and that of others around them – but there were also bibles of domesticity available to offer information, such as Mrs Beeton's *Book of Household Management*. Published in 1861, her advice was still being followed well into the twentieth century. 'Polish for the boots is an important matter to the valet, and not always to be obtained good by purchase; never so good, perhaps, as he can make for himself after the following recipe: Take of ivory-black and treacle each 4oz, sulphuric acid 1oz, best olive-oil 2 spoonfuls, best white-wine vinegar 3 half-pints: mix the ivory-black and treacle well in an earthen jar; then add the sulphuric acid, continuing to stir the mixture; next pour in the oil; and, lastly, add the vinegar, stirring it in by degrees, until thoroughly incorporated.'

Tricks of the trade

Charles Dean went to work for the Duke of Beaufort at Badminton, in 1920, as second footman. While there he was taught by the under butler, Jimmy Weedon, how to clean silver: 'For him it was a ritual. He had two lead sinks; in one he had a mixture of soft soap and water and whisked it until it had a good froth; this he made in the morning and it lay there all day, being occasionally replenished. In the other sink he rinsed the silver under the hot tap, then transferred it to the soapy water, returned it and rinsed it in cold. Then he would lay it on the draining board on its side: it could stay there all day and not get smeary. When it was required he would throw a jug of hot water over it, wipe it and it was perfect.'

Authur Shuttlewood 18 BRAMPTON ROAD
RIPON.

Tips from the Servants' Hall

- Clean satin ball slippers by rubbing them with breadcrumbs.
- Fill red wine glasses with warm water so stains can't develop before they are properly washed.
- Use soda to get marks out of a collar.
- Salt of sorrel will clean copper pots.
- Scour copper bowls with water and vinegar to get a high shine.
- Split card laid beneath brass buttons will protect the coat when polishing them.
- Wrap a delicate evening coat in linen when sewing on a missing button.

MARY

'Women like me don't have a life. We choose clothes
and pay calls and work for charity and do the Season.
But really we're stuck in a waiting room until we marry.'

Elizabeth McGovern is Cora

'Mary is a very well-written typical eldest child in that she puts her own needs at the forefront ... She's not as inclined to conciliate or placate. Cora is fascinated by Mary.'

The daughters of the house – Mary, Edith and Sybil – find it hardest of all to carve out a role for themselves. In 1912 it was difficult for women to enjoy any kind of independence until they were married. While living under their father's roof, they are subject to his rules. Fortunately, Cora and Robert are interested parents and Cora, as an American, might enjoy her children's company more than her British counterparts would have done. Still, the girls' time is mainly spent preparing themselves for a successful marriage. A governess was employed to teach French and possibly German. Then the girls would have been trained to start conversations, in preparation for their coming social duties with tongue-tied inferiors. Julian recalls that members of his own family had precisely this sort of instruction, 'My great-aunts would be taken round the gardens by their governess and at every shrub they would have to introduce a new subject. The idea was that you could keep a conversation going even with someone who was completely socially incapable.' On top of all this, any musical skill was always a bonus; playing the piano and singing – though only ever for private entertainments. Painting in watercolours was considered an asset (not, as a rule, oils, which were considered a little Bohemian), and embroidery and decoupage were encouraged.

Like all sisters, the girls can be arguing fiercely one minute and loyally defending each other the next. Edith, squashed between the beautiful Mary and the ambitious Sybil, sets herself up in competition with her elder sister, scheming to win their battle to land a suitable husband. Mary, as the first born, feels the pressure to get the very best husband possible; when potentially brilliant suitors appear to be making overtures to Mary, the whole household is on tenterhooks.

When not plotting invitations to eligible sons, writing carefully worded letters to them, or practising any of the skills that are supposed to improve their marriage prospects, the girls spend most of their time changing their outfits throughout the course of the day. The choosing of skirts and accessories, finding clever ways to update details and trying out new hairstyles, turns the chore of dressing into something rather more pleasant. At least this side of life is unashamedly fun when they are all together and getting on well, gossiping with each other and the maids, who are helping them dress. At all other times, the lives of the daughters and the servants could not be further apart, but in those moments they share in the simple delight of being young girls together.

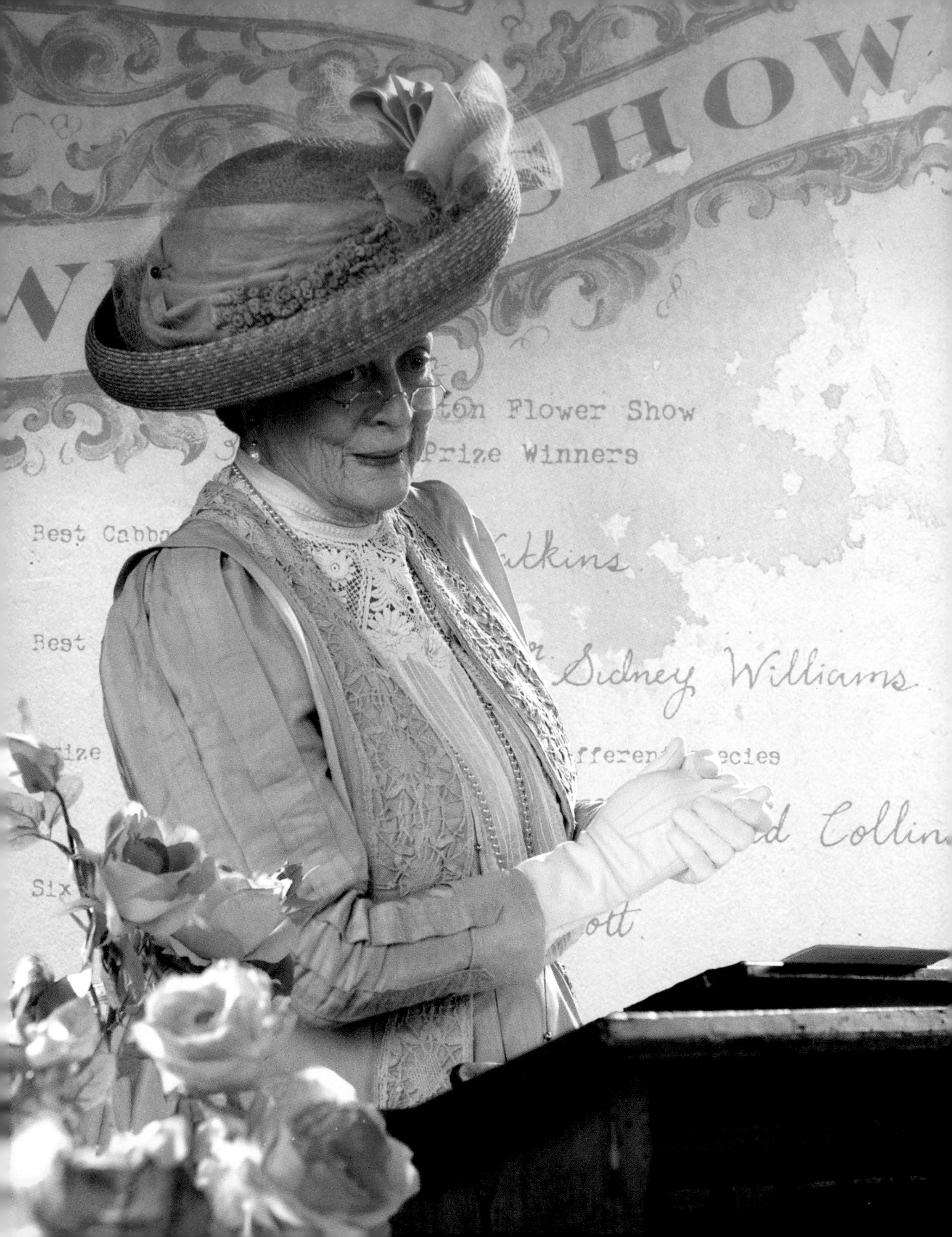
SHOW
Flower Show
Prize Winners
Sidney Williams

Society

CHAPTER TWO

Mary: 'I hope you're not dreading it too much?'

Robert: 'Not dreading it exactly, but it's a brave
new world we're headed for, no doubt about that;
we must try to meet it with as much grace
as we can muster ...'

To be truly accepted into Society at the turn of the last century, you had to be born into it. While there were books published on etiquette, there were pages and pages more of unwritten rules that should be observed – and a knowledge of these marked out those who were grand as opposed to those who were not. For someone like Violet, the Dowager Countess, the notion of her world changing and allowing a broader cross-section of people to enter it was insupportable. Some things were preordained and immutable: Society, and the circle of people who encompassed it, was one of them.

Violet is an aristocrat through and through and, as a firm believer in *noblesse oblige*, is committed to its principles. Although aware of the changes occurring, or threatening to occur, in the younger generation's way of life, Violet nevertheless believes that the rules of Society are fixed. So when she is faced with a middle-class interloper, with his 'weekends' and his bicycles, taking over her late husband's family's title and estate, she expects that the sheer might of her aristocratic power and privilege will win out and preserve the status quo.

However, the situation is not as bleak as Violet would paint it; although he has a lot to learn when it comes to the subtle politics of life as a nobleman, Matthew is not a man without social standing. He is, in fact, a part of the prosperous, professional upper-middle class. Brought up in Manchester by well-educated parents, he could certainly conduct himself with ease in even the upper tiers of Society – he can ride and is affronted when Thomas infers that he may not know how to serve himself

VIOLET, THE DOWAGER COUNTESS

'I have plenty of friends I don't like.'

ISOBEL CRAWLEY

'*What should we call each other?*'

VIOLET, THE DOWAGER COUNTESS

'*We could always start with*
Mrs Crawley and Lady Grantham.'

Violet, the Dowager Countess

'Violet believes that if you take a brick out of the aristocratic wall the whole thing comes crumbling down', says Julian Fellowes. Violet knows that she can do nothing about Matthew Crawley inheriting Lord Grantham's title – in 1912 there was no legal mechanism in place which would enable someone to renounce a peerage – but she decides she must do all she can to save Cora's money for Mary, if not the whole estate itself. As she herself said: 'Mary holds a trump card. Mary is family.' After all, Violet worked for years to keep the estate going and continues to live on it as the Dowager Countess; she cannot allow this remote cousin to threaten the formidable walls of prestige that buttress her own existence.

Authur Shuttlewood 18 BRAMPTON ROAD
RIPON.

at dinner. Yet Matthew is also a liberal: he understands the argument put forward by the suffragettes and is sympathetic to their cause. He is on the side of social change and so when he discovers he is to inherit a new position in the higher ranks of Society, as an earl with a great estate, he does not immediately feel it is a good thing. Matthew is not socially ambitious, but his feelings are irrelevant; whatever happens he *will* become an earl, what matters is how he handles this transition.

More sympathetic to Matthew's plight is Cora, who, as an American, is well versed in the treatment meted out to outsiders. Her mother-in-law has, after all, managed to be insufferable to her for 24 years. While Cora is educated in the strange ways of the English upper classes and has adopted most of them as her own, she is not a snob and she does not denigrate people who try to make their own way in the world. 'I can't see why he has the right to your estate or my money,' Cora tells Robert later. 'But I refuse to condemn him for wanting an honest job.'

MATTHEW
'I still don't see why I couldn't just refuse it.'

ISOBEL CRAWLEY
'There is no mechanism for you to do so! You will *be an earl. You* will *inherit the estate.'*

Cora's story is a familiar one amongst the English aristocracy at the time. She was part of a wave of eligible American girls who came to Britain from the late 1870s for the next 50 years; they were known as the 'Buccaneers'. These girls were often daughters of self-made men who had originated in the backwaters of America but had now left that life behind them with newfound wealth. Having made their money and built opulent houses, these entrepreneurs wanted to secure their daughters' futures with good marriages. They wanted the thing that money couldn't buy: class.

But there was just one problem. The upper echelons of Society in Virginia or Wisconsin, let alone New York, were almost impenetrable.

Usually there was a formidable society hostess at the top, and she would decide whether you were in or out. If there was even a hint of scandal in the past or your family was not deemed 'old' enough, you weren't in – and there was very little you could do to get there. So the more determined matriarchs made their way to Europe, where the aristocrats were secure enough in their titles and estates to welcome the pretty, rich and fun young women to the party. And, they liked the smell of the American girls' money. One of the earliest of these matriarchs leading the wave across the Atlantic was the mother of Jennie Jerome. She managed to secure a noble marriage for her daughter to Lord Randolph Churchill, which gave Jennie her entrée into Society. Their son was Winston, who became the famous wartime Prime Minister.

MARY

'You're American. You don't understand these things.'

Cora, the daughter of Isidore Levinson, a dry goods millionaire from Cincinnati, arrived in England in 1888, when she was 20 years old, with her mother as chaperone. By this time, even respectable rich American girls preferred to find their husbands amongst the nobility. Thanks to the successes of the earlier Buccaneers and a fashion for all things European, from interiors to dress designers such as the House of Worth, pursuing an English marriage had now become desirable. For these families, the many years in which Americans had fought to escape the clutches of colonial rule and create their own republic appeared to have been forgotten.

In fact, even the early Buccaneers found that getting a title was positively easy: many members of the English upper classes had fallen on hard times and they needed American money to bail them out and secure their estates. In order to achieve such a match, Cora's mother knew she had to ensure that her only daughter made the best possible entrance into Society. There was only one way to do this: to get presented at Court.

This wasn't as difficult as it sounds – while the daughters of dukes and earls obviously had an easy route in, the net of invitees was thrown

American heiresses

Unlike their English counterparts across the pond, American women were able to be – and frequently were – the heiresses to their fathers' millions. As a general rule, the American rich divide their money between their children (which is why so few American fortunes last), meaning the daughters of a rich man are wealthy in their own right. Consuelo Vanderbilt was an American heiress who famously married into the Marlborough dukedom, bringing with her a dowry of $9 million, an almost unbelievable sum at the time, even though she had two perfectly healthy brothers. This would never have happened in England.

...ntess of Grantham

...nton Abbey,

...ownton,

Yorkshire.

Learning your place in Society

The intricacies of aristocratic etiquette were explained to Consuelo Vanderbilt by her husband's friend, Lady Lansdowne, and came as a shock to her more informal sensibilities: 'I gathered from her conversation that an English lady was hedged round with what seemed to me to be boring restrictions. It appeared that one should not walk alone in Piccadilly or in Bond Street, nor sit in Hyde Park unless accompanied ... that it was better to occupy a box than a stall at the theatre, and that to visit a music-hall was out of the question. One must further be careful not to be compromised, and at a ball one should not dance twice with the same man. One must learn to take one's place in the social hierarchy ... One must, in other words, learn the "Peerage" [the book that lists all the noble families in Britain] ... Indeed my first contact with society in England brought with it a realisation that it was fundamentally a hierarchical society in which the differences in rank were outstandingly important.'

relatively wide. There were three criteria: you had to be a girl of upstanding morals, you had to be introduced by someone who had themselves been presented (you could arrange this for a fee with some of the less scrupulous former debutantes); and you had to be either aristocratic or of the 'ranks' – the amorphous body which included the clergy, military, merchants, bankers and large-scale commerce dealers. Once presented, Cora would have enjoyed a packed Season (her daughters would later attend the same parties, with almost all the same families) – in itself a thinly veiled excuse for husband-hunting.

However, despite the enthusiasm with which these rich American girls were welcomed onto English shores, Cora's entry into Society would not have been entirely easy. While there were those who courted her because of her beauty and in the hope of a slice of her cash-rich pie, there were more who would have looked down their noses at her too-fashionable dresses, her lack of knowledge of the finer points of etiquette and her American nationality itself. Without much help, Cora would have had to learn quickly the English way of doing things – even if she already thought she knew which fork to use and how to compose a menu. She would, for example, have been thrown by the fact that while Americans were happy to introduce themselves, the English waited for a formal introduction, which for someone like her might not always have been forthcoming.

By the end of her first Season, Cora had become engaged to Robert, later Lord Grantham, who was in dire need of money to rescue his estate. Their marriage was born from convenience but grew into romance, as they fell in love the year after they married. But marriage to an earl did not mean that life would now be easy for Cora. Once settled into her new home, Cora would have found herself in a land that was almost alien to her upbringing. As the wife of a peeress, she would be entitled to wear velvet and ermine at coronations, as well as often taking the place of honour at dinners; her writing paper would bear the family crest and her bed sheets would be monogrammed.

Not all of the new elements would be welcome to someone who was an enlightened, educated and lively American girl. 'It also probably meant inheriting an ancestral home full of creaky ancestral machinery: shooting parties for which the guest list hadn't changed in three generations, family jewels that could not be reset no matter how ugly they were … Marrying the peer turned the heiress into an institution, incessantly compared to the last woman who'd held the job and, because she was

Elizabeth McGovern is Cora

'My approach to the part is about my own experiences as an American living in England. Things aren't addressed in conversation openly, but by inference, nuance and understanding.'

American, frequently found wanting,' wrote Gail MacColl and Carol Wallace in *To Marry An English Lord*. In an enormous house miles away from the excitement of London, let alone the vast ocean that separated her from her family and friends, Cora would have been inhuman not to have felt lonely and bewildered in the early days of marriage.

'I mean, one way or another, everyone goes down the aisle with half the story hidden.'

Fortunately, Robert is a kind man and became a loving husband: one who would be a much-needed pacifier between his wife and mother. Violet did not change her views and decide to be more welcoming of her daughter-in-law because, as Julian Fellowes explains: 'She understands about money but she sees aristocratic virtues as more important. She didn't encourage Robert's marriage where his father certainly did. She would rather have taken less of a dowry with someone who knew the ropes better.' Above all, Cora failed to provide a son, and as the years went by this would have diminished her to almost nothing in Violet's eyes. According to Julian: 'The lack of a son is an issue. In those days the selection of the sex – in fact, anything "defective" about a child – was thought to be the woman's fault. By definition, of course, your mother-in-law had always managed to have a son.'

Without a son, as we know, the matter of the passing on of the title and Downton Abbey is greatly affected. On marriage, Cora's sizeable dowry and later inheritance had been wrapped up tightly within the estate. This was not unusual; primogeniture – when only the eldest male heir may inherit – was a law that had ring-fenced the British aristocracy for hundreds of years. Tied up with it was the policy of entail, which meant that estates were bound in trust so they could only be passed on whole from one generation to the next, which ensured all the ancient properties remained intact, preventing bits being divided off and sold or given away to any other person. Younger sons or daughters could never inherit more than a token amount of cash or trinkets: the house and its contents – from jewels to paintings and furniture – and all its land would go solely to the next male heir. Usually that was the eldest son, but when

THE REAL-LIFE CORA: LADY CURZON

The idea for Cora was born when Julian Fellowes read about Mary Leiter in *To Marry An English Lord*, by Gail MacColl and Carol Wallace. Mary (right), was a dark-haired beauty, the daughter of a fantastically rich Chicago real estate speculator and a very vulgar, ambitious mother. Riding on the crest of the Buccaneer wave, Mary came to Europe following social success in Washington, New York and Newport. However, she failed to make much of an impression during several visits in the late 1880s, until 1890, when in a single day she met the Prince of Wales (later King Edward VII and a well-known champion of American girls), a Duchess and a former Prime Minister. Later that Season she went to a ball, entering as 'a statuesque beauty in a stupendous Worth gown' and the Prince of Wales asked to have his first dance with her.

After that, she was made: invited by the inner London social circles to every luncheon, dinner and ball. Men were throwing themselves at her feet, but she had fallen in love with the Honourable George Curzon (right), a very bright but equally broke young man. He, too, had certainly noticed her at that first ball but, afraid that to propose to her would be too obviously a fortune-hunter's move, he held back. In the summer of 1891 they saw each other every day but his feelings remained ambiguous. Mary waited for him for years, always believing he would come to her, despite only measured responses from him. Even when he did propose in 1893 he told her to keep the engagement secret, leaving her mother wondering impatiently why her daughter was yet to marry despite her numerous suitors. Only in 1895 did he finally talk to her father and his, and then they were married.

Her father bought them a house – 1 Carlton House Terrace – and gave them £6000 a year. He also settled a sum rumoured to be somewhere between $700,000 and $1 million on Mary, with an additional amount set aside for any children they might have (they had three daughters: Irene, Cynthia and Alexandra – the last was born in 1904).

While Mary had always been utterly in love with George – she once said that when he came through a door, she felt 'that the band is playing the Star Spangled Banner and that the room is glowing with pink lights and rills are running up and down [my] back with joy' – it was only after he had been posted to India as Viceroy, three years after their marriage, that he came to love her with equal fervour. Sadly, just over ten years after their wedding she grew ill in India and died, in 1906. But she died a happily married woman and, as Vicereine of India, the highest-ranking American, man or woman, in the history of the British Empire.

Sisters

All of the actresses playing Mary, Edith and Sybil have only sisters in their families.

no son was forthcoming, as in Cora and Robert's case, it went to the nearest male relation. So while her mother had been an heiress, Mary could not be. Even to her, steeped as she was in the traditions and expectations of her class, this was beyond the pale: 'I don't believe a woman can be forced to give all her money to a distant cousin of her husband's. Not in the twentieth century. It's too ludicrous for words.'

Yet even in a remote seat like Downton Abbey, Cora is not bereft of influence, as the aristocracy tended to be a matriarchy. Downton is one of the great houses of England, and if anyone locally wants an invitation or support for a project, it is Cora that they have to get on their side. As a peeress, she could invite several young men to the house on any one of her daughters' behalf, because most of their mothers would be only too pleased to be thought of as a friend. Her only difficulty would be that there weren't all that many available. 'I'm afraid we're rather a female party tonight, Duke,' she explains when the raffish Duke of Crowborough is staying. 'But you know what it's like trying to balance numbers in the country. A single man outranks the Holy Grail.' (A sentiment that many a country hostess would feel even in the twenty-first century.)

Perhaps her most modern achievement has been to imbue her daughters with the sense that power is theirs for the taking. The only difference is in the manner with which they take it. 'Mary wants power but is prepared to play by the old rules,' says Julian. 'Sybil wants it by the new rules. And Edith just wants anything she can get.'

As the girls reach eighteen, the time arrives for them to 'Come Out'. For Cora's daughters, their entry into Society as debutantes took a more simple route than that of their mother; as aristocracy they had an automatic 'in' that had been denied Cora. The Season was their opportunity to meet the right circle of men from which to choose a husband. 'For marriage market it was,' writes Anna Sproule of this annual ritual in *The Social Calendar*. 'Nobody in the pre-1914 era made any bones about the fact that marriage was a woman's sole career, and she owed it both to herself and the family that had so far supported her to get on with it.'

The girls' entrée into Society would begin, as it had for their mother, with their presentation at Court. Despite the different years in which they were presented, each of the daughters would have worn more or less the same outfit for the occasion: a long, low gown and three ostrich feathers pinned to their head (a dictat of King Edward VII), a veil and a decent length of train.

SYBIL

'There's nothing wrong with doctors.
We all need doctors.'

MARY

'We all need crossing sweepers and draymen, too.
It doesn't mean we have to dine with them.'

Presentation would be followed by the Season, which traditionally began with the Royal Academy Summer Exhibition. With no shooting or hunting at that time of year, and the men in London to attend Parliament, they were available to escort their wives and daughters around the social whirligig. Four thousand of the richest and smartest people in England descended on the capital from the end of April to the latter part of July for the Covent Garden opera season, the Eton and Harrow cricket match, Royal Ascot (in 1910 everyone wore black mourning for the King who had died the month before), lawn tennis at various venues, including Wimbledon, the Henley Regatta, and a series of garden receptions, private concerts, balls, dinners, receptions and just plain parties.

LADY ROSAMUND

'I'm sorry you haven't received more invitations. But then, after four Seasons, one is less a debutante than a survivor.'

The Season was really all about parties, especially those given in the great London palaces, which many of the most significant families still owned and lived in. They would host enormous gatherings every night and every day the newspapers would report who had been present, as well as who had hosted what the previous night – who went and who was giving the next one. Essentially it was an endless succession of opportunities for young people to meet and for their parents to catch up. Even in the daylight hours there was no time lost in finding a way to see and be seen, as young men and women on horseback cantered up and down Hyde Park's Rotten Row for exercise.

Come 12 August, the grouse season opened in Scotland and everyone shut up their London houses again. You had to hope that by that time you had already caught your future husband as securely as a salmon on a fly hook.

To make her mark, a girl had to be pretty, finely dressed and of excellent parentage. Mothers chaperoned their daughters everywhere, sizing each other up across the dance floor. They would be assessing the competition, as well as the potential suitability of their daughters' beaux. No

The ceremony of 'Coming Out'

In 1911, Lady Diana Manners (right), the third daughter of the 8th Duke of Rutland, was presented at Court: 'I had made my own train – three yards of cream net sprinkled generously with pink rose-petals, each attached by a diamond dewdrop. The dress was adequate and the three feathers springing out of my head looked less ridiculous when everyone was wearing them... I was nervous of making my double curtsy. The courtiers are very alarming and martinettish – they shoo you and pull you back and speak to you as they would to a wet dog, but once the trial is successfully over you have the fun of seeing others go through the same ordeal.'

THE REAL-LIFE SIR RICHARD CARLISLE: LORDS BEAVERBROOK AND NORTHCLIFFE

Sir Richard Carlisle is loosely based on the newspaper magnates who made their fortunes out of the First World War. The Canadian tycoon Max Aitken, later Lord Beaverbrook, was a prominent figure largely because of his political friends as well as his rousing leaders in the *Daily Express*. But it was Lord Northcliffe who led the way in tabloid journalism with the establishment of the *Daily Mirror* and the *Daily Mail* – his descendant, Lord Rothermere, is still the majority shareholder of his newspaper group.

Aitken is compelling for his political bombast. A protégé of the Conservative party leader, Bonar Law (who formed the wartime coalition government with Lloyd George), and a friend of Winston Churchill, his personal alliances guided his newspaper editorials, which were hugely influential in directing politics after the war. But it was the brash effrontery of Lord Northcliffe, born Alfred Harmsworth in Dublin to 'a tough mother and a feckless hard-drinking father' in 1865, that could be said to be responsible for influencing some of the major decisions of the war cabinet, including – with Beaverbrook's *Express* – the destruction of the Liberal government.

When the *Daily Mail* was first printed in 1896, the immediate effect was electrifying. Gone were the word-for-word dull reports of political speeches; in were first-person accounts of events. Easy on the eye with lots of white space on the page and an early use of big pictures, one could say that the founding principles still operate on the paper today. 'The three things which are always news are health things, sex things and money things,' Northcliffe told a reporter. Cheap to buy and titillating to read, the paper made him a millionaire. Northcliffe died in 1922 quite mad, probably due to a blood infection, and a newspaper man to the end; he telephoned his night editor and told him: 'They say that I am mad: send your best man to cover the story.'

The Daily

one could be seen to dance with the same man for the whole evening, so the opportunities to gauge whether you liked him or not were scant. Instead, opinions were formed on the gossip and stories that related to his fortune, background and character. Naturally enough, the men did the same about the women.

Not that a deb's troubles were over once she had 'caught' a fiancé. Any potential husband would be checked out by both the family and the servants. When Mary brings home Sir Richard Carlisle, he is seen as the classic *arriviste* and there is consternation in the ranks. But he enters their lives in the middle of the war: all around them there is change, and Society is changing too, as impossible as that had seemed to the older generations. Bringing with him money and confidence, Sir Richard is unfazed by the stuffy ways of the Crawleys. He is happy to do his best to fit in with the grand country family (he orders a country suit to go walking in) but is unembarrassed when he doesn't quite manage it (he has mistakenly ordered a heavy tweed more suited to shooting). As unpalatable as he may be at times, Sir Richard represents the future – a way into power that doesn't depend on blue-blooded connections but an agile mind and ambitious drive instead.

With new pathways to the top of Society being laid in this decade, Matthew may feel the pressure to be a pioneer on top of his duty to Lord Grantham to preserve the traditions of Downton Abbey. His future earldom will give him a seat in the House of Lords but it might be, after all, his upper middle-class background and professional career that enable him to make his peerage a success rather than, as Violet and Lord Grantham fear, hold him back.

Change

CHAPTER THREE

TIMELINE

1913

The suffragette movement continued to claim headlines when Emily Davison ran out in front of the King's horse at the Epsom Derby in June. She died of her wounds a few days later, but she lived on in the minds of many as a controversial figure whose actions may, in fact, have blighted the suffragette cause.

1912

On 17 January Captain Scott and his team successfully reached the South Pole, only to perish in March as they made their way home. On 15 April, tragedy struck again when the 'unsinkable' ocean liner RMS *Titanic* hit an iceberg on her maiden voyage across the Atlantic. It sank within hours, killing over 1500 people, mostly men from first and second and passengers from third class. The summer brought more scandal as the British government was accused of profiting from information about the Marconi Company.

1915

1915 saw no let up in hostilities, and for the first time London suffered the effects of the First World War directly when streets were hit by Zeppelins. Meanwhile, Britain tried to carry on as normal, bringing in change in these shifting times. In this year photographs were required on passports for the first time, and the Women's Institute was formed in response to the demands made on women to help the war effort.

1914

The assassination of Archduke Franz Ferdinand of Austria in June 1914 by a Serb nationalist heralded the start of tensions between the two nations. As other countries across Europe took sides, military momentum gathered that could only lead to the announcement of the First World War and Britain's call to arms.

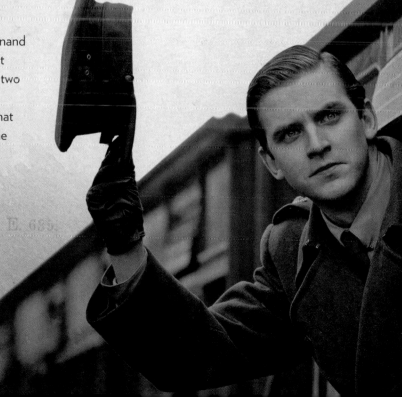

Army Form E. 689.

rritorial Force.

BODIMENT.

OTICE TO JOIN

1916

July brought the commencement of the Battle of the Somme; an offensive by British and French armies against the German Army which lasted until November. It became one of the bloodiest military operations ever recorded, causing over 1.5 million casualties, with over 60,000 British soldiers lost in the first day alone. Over in Dublin, Irish republicans mounted an insurrection during Easter week, aiming to end British Rule in Ireland. The Easter Rising was suppressed after seven days but succeeded in bringing the issue to the forefront of Irish politics. As the year drew to a close, back home the Prime Minister, H.H. Asquith, lost the support and confidence of the press and his government and resigned his position in December. He was succeeded by David Lloyd George.

1917

After the dramatic losses sustained during the Battle of the Somme, 1917 saw another, equally horrific battle take place, notorious for the horrendous conditions endured by the troops. Passchendaele saw fighting from July until November in the muddy quagmire of Ypres, resulting in heavy casualties. After a failed harvest back in Britain, the Government's Food Production Department swiftly set up the Women's Land Army, which mobilised women in farming to ensure food reserves could supply the nation.

1918

A year of great changes began with the passing of the Representation of the People Act, which finally gave women the vote – if they were over 30 and owned property – as well as to men in residence over the age of 21. Food supplies continued to be regulated with the introduction of ration books. In Russia, the incarceration of the Russian royal family came to an end when the Bolsheviks executed them in a panic on 16 July, believing that Czech forces were on their way to rescue them. On 11 November the news came that everyone had been waiting for – the Allies had won the war and the Germans had signed the armistice that ended the conflict.

1919

Six months of negotiations finally concluded with the signing of the Treaty of Versailles, in which Germany was forced to accept responsibility for the war and to make reparations to many countries involved in the conflict. Britain celebrated with victory parades across the country. There was more cause for celebration when, on 15 June, John Alcock and Arthur Whitten Brown made history as they completed the first non-stop flight across the Atlantic Ocean.

WASTE NOT–WANT NOT

PREPARE FOR WINTER

Save
Perishable Foods
by
Preserving Now

At dawn, a steam train travels through this lovely part of England. As the camera moves in, we can see a man, whom we will know as John Bates, sitting by himself in a third-class carriage. Above him run the telephone wires, humming with their unrevealed, urgent messages. The train flies on.

ur first glimpse of Bates shows a man on his way to a new job, a man with a purpose. In many ways he is not so unlike people these days: dressed in a smart outfit, travelling by train with an appointment to make. Yet it is his new job title, personal valet to Lord Grantham of Downton Abbey, that separates his world from ours. Almost from the moment that we meet him, however, his way of life begins to change.

In 1912, Sybil is 17 years old and poised on the brink of adulthood. Having shed the cares of her juvenile years, she wonders what the next decade will bring. While her sisters have begun to map out their lives according to a pattern laid down by their ancestors – doing the Season to procure an engagement to someone titled and rich, followed by marriage, a few children and hopefully little more to concern them beyond charity work, promoting the interests of her family, and concocting guest lists – Sybil does not want to tread this well-worn path. As it happens, so far at any rate, neither Mary's nor Edith's lives are turning out quite as they hoped, but their destinies are not entirely within their control. For everyone in Britain, the decade leading up to 1920 saw great shifts in society.

Life at the turn of the twentieth century was not so different from our own a hundred years later. Just as ongoing developments in technology influence the way we communicate, travel, live and work now, the Edwardians laboured to adapt to the fast, furious arrival of abundant inventions. Violet and her generation feel they are living in an increasingly foreign world as electric lights, telephones and motor cars affect

Howard's End, by E.M. Forster (1910)

'Railway termini ... are our gates to the glorious and the unknown. Through them we pass out into adventure and sunshine, to them, alas! we return.'

No. 3.   General   Hospital at Saint Pair
         Stationary

ARMY FORM

Regtl. No.   Date 21 - 7 - 18

Name

Regt. or Corps.

Name of Ship

their lives in ways they could never have envisaged even ten years before, even if they don't always recognise it at once. A telephone, for example, might be an exciting new contraption in the house, but the likes of Carson and Mrs Hughes do not see what difference it can make beyond the footmen no longer having to walk into the village to deliver a message or send a telegram.

Sybil, however, with her youthful hope and curiosity, is ready to take on all the challenges that the new decade will bring. Shedding herself of the expectations of her class and sex, she eagerly embraces the new ideas. With nobody to share her progressive theories, she finds a sympathetic ear in an unlikely source – Branson, the chauffeur. An Irish radical, Branson sees no reason for living according to the old rules and wants to bring about change in the social order. He believes that, together, he and Sybil can persuade those around them of the importance and sense of political reformation.

Despite her enthusiasm, Sybil does understand that for many of the family and servants it is difficult to believe that real change is possible; she wants change just as much as Branson but she sees more clearly the challenges that lie ahead. Her grandmother, Violet, the Dowager Countess, views any innovation as an affront to the very social order that God established, and even Robert and Cora find it hard to envision any new idea lasting beyond the caprice of youth.

But change did come and it left the rules of the previous decade in its wake. In their place grew Socialism, women's rights, improved healthcare and technological advances. The war was one catalyst that brought about these breakthroughs, but there were several other factors that came into play, from economics to science. One of the first drivers was the introduction of death duties in 1894 – these rose again in 1909 and 1919, and the great estates no longer could be handed to the next generation without enormous payments to the Government. Further squeezes to the funds of the upper classes were felt through sharp rises in income tax and servants' wages. Robert doubtless would have had many more sleepless nights had it not been for his fortunate marriage to Cora, whose large inheritance supplemented their income. Without it, the survival of Downton Abbey would have been questionable.

Many of Robert's fellow country house families were not so lucky and struggled to keep going after the war, ultimately being forced to sell up. Only the new rich – men who had made their money in newspapers, oil,

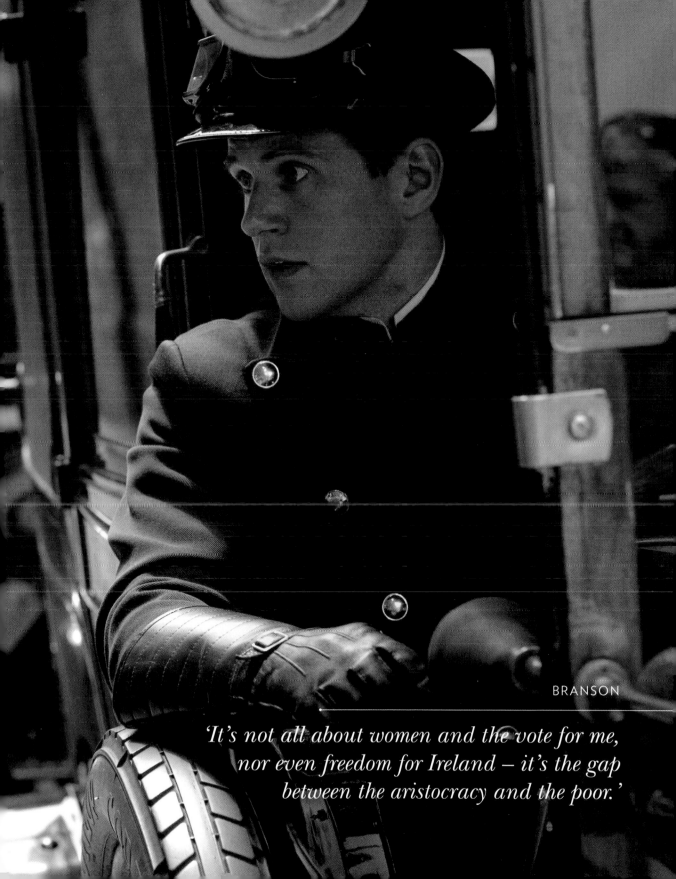

BRANSON

'It's not all about women and the vote for me,
nor even freedom for Ireland – it's the gap
between the aristocracy and the poor.'

the City and manufacturing – could afford to buy these once-hereditary estates. Nor was this change of hands the only adjustment that the estates would undergo; the number of people working in service started to decrease sharply and few places ran the same levels of staffing they would have done even 20 years before. More labour-saving devices, too, meant that vast numbers of servants were no longer required to perform certain roles in the running of the house.

At the same time, there was a new generation of workers who no longer believed that entering service was their best option. Gwen shows considerable courage in daring to wish that she might work as a secretary one day – she goes against everything her parents and their ancestors had done before her. But she is not alone. Other servants, too, begin to question the path that has been laid out before them. Politics fires their dreams, but the fuel also comes from their improved literacy and the ideas they get from going to the new cinema picture houses. Thomas, O'Brien, Rose and Ethel would once have been content to stay in service – if not for their entire careers, at least until they got married – and they would have thought themselves well-off for it. Not any more.

ETHEL

'Why shouldn't she learn to cook and scrub? She may need it when the war's over. Things are changing. For her lot and us, and when they do I mean to make the most of it.'

Against this fluctuating climate, Liberal Prime Minister H.H. Asquith, with David Lloyd George as Chancellor of the Exchequer, worked hard to engineer several key domestic reforms, including the introduction of old-age pensions and National Insurance. The voice of the poor working man was beginning to be heard: power was no longer the preserve of the blue-blooded. By 1922 it was possible for Bonar Law to be elected Prime Minister – a man who was neither aristocratic nor the owner of a country house.

The seeds of Socialism had been sown in the 1880s, but it took until the turn of the century for them to flourish. In 1900 the Labour Representation Committee was formed and by 1906, 29 'Labour'

Amy Nuttall is Ethel

'Ethel has come from working for a very small household where she was just one of two housemaids, so it's an achievement for her to get the job at Downton, but I don't think she realises she's so fortunate. She wants more ... and her behaviour doesn't go down too well.'

THE DAWN OF HOPE.

Mr. LLOYD GEORGE'S National Health Insurance Bill provi[...]
of the Worker in case of Sickness.

Support the Liberal Gove[...]
in their policy of
SOCIAL REFORM

The

Socialist Party

v.

The Liberal
Party

[...]ould the Working Class support the

Liberal Party?"

FACTS FOR
SOCIALISTS

No. 1

FACTS FOR
SOCIALISTS
From the Political
Economists and
Statisticians.

Eleventh Edition (Revised)

[...]AILY CITIZEN

candidates won seats in the General Election. Once ensconsed, the Committee renamed themselves the Labour Party and revealed a manifesto that demanded seats for 'the people' in the House of Commons, and which would fight for the rights of Trade Unions, the aged poor, shopkeepers and traders. 'Wars are fought to make the rich richer, and underfed schoolchildren are neglected,' they proclaimed. But even the well-educated and empowered Liberals, who counted the aristocrat Winston Churchill amongst them, had their own firebrands. Prime Minister Asquith, who had toppled 14 years of Tory rule in 1906, was certainly one, but Lloyd George, when campaigning for his new budget in 1909, was notable for his 'incendiary wit'.

LORD GRANTHAM

'And Mr Lloyd George's new insurance measures will help.'

VIOLET, THE DOWAGER COUNTESS

'Please don't speak that man's name, we are about to eat.'

Needing £8 million to fund new battleships and another £8 million to save people from the workhouse and to pay pensions for those in poverty, Lloyd George proposed raising the necessary finances through higher income tax, estate duties, alcohol and tobacco duties and a rising tax from cars and petrol. There was also a 'super tax' and 'land tax' put forward; despite the fact that less than a hundred thousand people would qualify for these taxes, they were, unfortunately for him, the people of influence. There was strong opposition to these measures, but Lloyd George rallied a large crowd at Limehouse, in the heart of London's Docklands and one of the poorest areas in the East End, on a hot night in July 1909. The landlords had threatened to sack labourers if the People's Budget was passed, but Lloyd George dismissed this as a hollow threat – what, he asked, would these landowners do in the Season without their staff? 'No weekend shooting with the Duke of Norfolk or anyone.' The speech gained supporters and enemies for the budget in almost equal measure, but the proposal was rejected by the House of

Lords (which was made up largely of Tory peers), leading to a constitutional crisis that forced two general elections the following year.

Despite the Government's hard-fought battles, there was a long way to go to bring about social reforms. Poverty remained an unrelenting problem. In 1912, one child in 12 at Britain's state schools was suffering from disease or the effects of poor diet. Of the six million schoolchildren across the country, more than half were in need of dental treatment and a third were described as 'unhygienically dirty'. Meanwhile, the Trade Unions flexed their muscles: striking dockers and miners caused riots and there was talk of a coming revolution, which saw upper-class men rushing to buy revolvers to protect themselves in their London clubs. Despite objections from these quarters, Parliament conceded the unions' demands. They were, after all, modest: another penny or two on the hourly rate, fair differentials, an eight-hour working day, free school meals for their children and a meagre but guaranteed old-age pension.

The tragic sinking of the RMS *Titanic* – the 'unsinkable ship' – in 1912 further highlighted the injustice of the old class system. Within hours two-thirds of the passengers had drowned in the icy waters of the North Atlantic, but there was outrage when it was later realised that first-class passengers had been put into the boats before others. In the worst example, the managing director of the owners, White Star Line, escaped in the last lifeboat, while only 20 of the 180 Irish passengers were saved.

LORD GRANTHAM

'God help the poor devils below decks, on their way to a better life. What a tragedy.'

Class distinctions in British society still remained, but slowly there were adjustments to the former order. The upper classes were no longer viewed with the same reverence and unquestioning respect, nor were the excesses of the rich as silently tolerated. The naughty antics of King Edward VII, with his lavish country house parties and his stream of married mistresses, were no longer setting the tone of behaviour in certain aristocratic sets. May 1910 had brought King George V to the Throne, a man who proved to be considerably more staid than his father, with his stamp-collecting and devotion to his wife, the stiff and severe Queen Mary.

Gareth Neame, Executive Producer

'We made a decision early on to open the series with the news about the loss of the *Titanic* as we felt that it was a very recognisable moment in history for the audience ... it reflects a change of gear for this sort of family, this life.'

TITANIC
DISASTER
GREAT LOSS
OF LIFE
EVENING NEWS

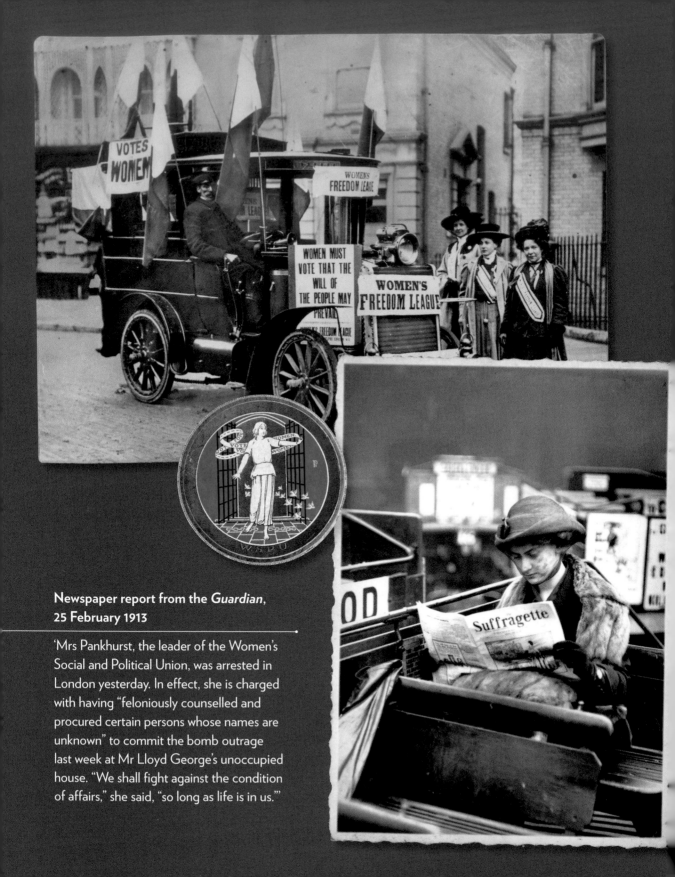

**Newspaper report from the *Guardian*,
25 February 1913**

'Mrs Pankhurst, the leader of the Women's
Social and Political Union, was arrested in
London yesterday. In effect, she is charged
with having "feloniously counselled and
procured certain persons whose names are
unknown" to commit the bomb outrage
last week at Mr Lloyd George's unoccupied
house. "We shall fight against the condition
of affairs," she said, "so long as life is in us."'

His prudishness meant that the peccadilloes of the Edwardian Court could no longer be tolerated.

The imbalances within society were not just driven by class or sex. Alongside women, some ordinary men were still denied the right to vote. This was because, although most of the property qualifications had been removed in the reforms of the 1870s, until 1918 a man who neither owned property nor paid any rent had no right to take part in general elections. This is something you would expect Thomas to mind greatly; as a domestic servant with no home of his own he cannot vote. But he prefers to worry about the things he can change, closer to home.

BRANSON

*'I never would have taken her there.
I may be a Socialist but I'm not a lunatic.'*

MARY

'I'm not sure Papa knows the difference.'

Women were not politically passive: many were active in organisations such as the Mother's Union and the Girls' Friendly Society. They canvassed, sat on school boards and were elected as local councillors, in which capacity they were responsible for introducing free school meals, subsidised milk and help for the elderly. Nor were women workshy; greater numbers were employed than perhaps might be assumed, and probably many more wished they could be. In the first decade of the twentieth century, 55 per cent of single women and 14 per cent of married women were engaged in paid jobs. Domestic service was still a big employer but was second choice for the likes of Gwen, particularly if they could be engaged as a secretary, factory worker or shopgirl in one of the bigger, glamorous department stores. Women were also employed in local government work, including teaching. By 1914, more than five million women were working (out of a population of 24 million women). Yet despite being entrusted with these positions and the ability to make important social decisions, women didn't have the right

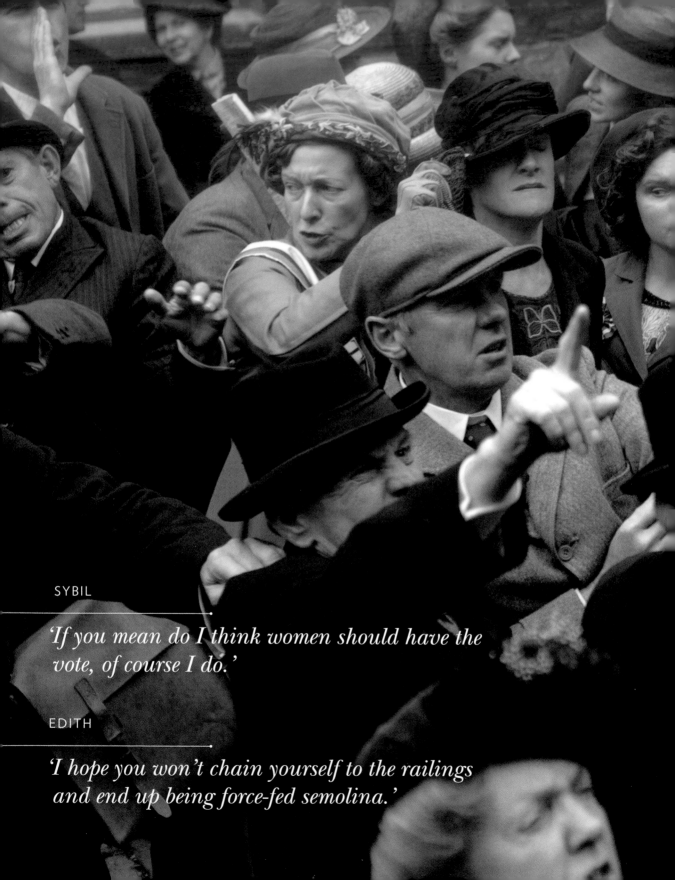

SYBIL

'If you mean do I think women should have the
vote, of course I do.'

EDITH

'I hope you won't chain yourself to the railings
and end up being force-fed semolina.'

to vote. Violet and Cora, as wives of peers, may not have thought about the right to vote (peers could not then elect members of the Commons) but Sybil, as a young girl, is rightly concerned with the question.

O'BRIEN

'Why does she waste her precious time on politics?'

While the greater part of the suffragette movement was campaigning through speeches, debates and other peaceable methods, a small group was spectacularly violent. Suffragette Lillian Lenton, who burned buildings as part of her protests, explained: 'Well, the object was to create an absolutely impossible state of affairs in the country, to prove that it was impossible to govern without the consent of the governed.' Politicians were personally attacked, windows were shattered and there were bloody clashes between the suffragettes and the police. This reached its peak in 1913, when Emily Davison ran out in front of the King's horse at the Derby and was killed.

During the war, most suffragettes agreed to put campaigning on hold so as not to distract the Government from matters of state, but the hardcore protestors decided to carry on. Violet's shock at Sybil's political views and Lord Grantham's fears for her safety are easier to understand when one reads about the brutal scenes that were taking place then. Despite the damaging work of a few extremists, the suffragettes did achieve their objective after the First World War. The roles of women during the war years had changed drastically, so much so that when the war was over, the Government acknowledged that it would not have been won without the efforts of the women.

For all that was deeply traditional about Downton Abbey, it could not escape the increasing mechanisation of daily life. The telephone was invented in 1876 by Alexander Graham Bell, a Scot living in America, and by 1879 there were 200 subscribers to the service in Britain. The first international service, between London and Paris, started in 1891. However, widespread adoption of the new-fangled device was fairly slow, thanks largely to regulations about the distances exchanges could serve and the Post Office's nervousness that it would lose valuable profit from

The militant suffragettes

Although Mildred Ransom was herself a
suffragette, she was rather shocked by the
difference between the constitutional suffragists
and the militants: 'They thought "frightfulness"
would terrify MPs into granting the reform.
They slashed Cabinet Ministers with dogwhips,
they set churches on fire, smashed plate-
glass windows of shops and poured acid into
pillarboxes, with the natural result that the
ordinary man in the street set his teeth against
granting any vote to any woman on any terms.'

Julian Fellowes

'The issue for Gareth [Gareth Neame, Executive Producer] and me at the very beginning of the idea was that we didn't want it to be in a kind of unrecognisable living experience. These were people with motor cars, trains and eventually telephones and electricity. So it was essentially modern.'

its telegram services. The first coin-operated call box was installed much later, in 1906, at Ludgate Circus in London, but by 1912, when the Postmaster-General took over the National Telephone Company with a multitude of exchanges and 1,500,000 miles of wire, Britain had its first unified system, catering for 561,738 subscribers across the country.

MRS PATMORE

'Oh, my Lord. Listen to that. It's like the cry of the banshee.'

Expansion of telephone services thereafter was rapid – much to Violet and Carson's dismay but everyone else's delight, particularly when the servants overhear the butler practising his 'telephone voice'.

In the house, electricity was another stimulus of change, not least because of the bright lights that now glared in the evening. This despite the fact that light from oil lamps and candles was undeniably prettier – the Marquess of Bath believed this so vehemently that he refused to install gas or electric light at Longleat, arguing that it would change the character of the rooms too much. Most homes took on electricity gradually, as Downton does, preferring to wait for teething problems with the new technology to be ironed out. Although the electric lightbulb was invented in 1878, early electrical systems were erratic and frequently dangerous, with plugs emitting sparks – at Hatfield, Lord Salisbury's family would hurl cushions up at sparks on the library ceiling.

Crucially, as electricity became more widely available so labour-saving devices became more common in homes and businesses. After the war, when there was a shortage of servants (mostly because they had been killed or seriously injured or had found more interesting work) these inventions went from being a luxury to a necessity. Gradually, the need for servants was reduced, which changed the way in which a country house was run. With the introduction of vacuum cleaners, gas fires and, later, washing machines and refrigerators (taking over from the outside meat safe), servants now had less work to do. An increasing number of factories produced canned, pickled and bottled foods, meaning that less of these staples had to be made at home. Commercial laundries and bakeries, too, picked up some of the domestics' workload. 'We look back quite nostalgically at a period when everyone knew what to wear and who was who and so on,' says Julian. 'But at the time one of the reasons for its demise was that everyone got bored with it. It was all so established and repetitive, and particularly when money was a bit tight, they thought how comfortable they could be in a smaller house with fewer servants.'

VIOLET, THE DOWAGER COUNTESS

'No, I couldn't have electricity in the house. I wouldn't sleep a wink. All those vapours seeping about.'

The advent of the motor car also changed daily life irrevocably. Although the carburettor mechanism had been in use since the 1860s, it was not until the early 1900s that production lines started to make cars in their thousands and at a more affordable price. In 1904 there were 8465 cars on the road; by 1910, there were 53,196. In 1912 the speed limit was raised from 14mph to 20mph, despite the fact that the first known fatality of a car killing a man on the street occurred at just 8mph. While the fast-growing train network, which began in the 1840s, meant people could travel cross-country in a matter of hours, cars made travelling locally and between town and country quick and easy. That is, for the rich; although prices were lower, cars were still the preserve of the comfortably off. In 1914 a four-cylinder car cost £750. To put this into relative terms, Prime Minister H.H. Asquith's salary that year was £5,000.

As use of the horse and carriage went out of fashion, coachmen and grooms were needed in fewer homes and in smaller numbers. Among the larger estates, horses didn't leave the stables altogether because the families would still ride for exercise or sport and traps would also be driven for pleasure around the grounds. In 1911, there were 67,228 domestic coachmen and grooms recorded on the population census and 25,151 motor drivers. Ten years later, the industrial sector of the census recorded 14,512 private coachmen and grooms and 25,857 motor drivers. The richer houses would employ several chauffeurs: at Cliveden there were five, including one each for Lord and Lady Astor.

While the young were thrilled with the opportunities that cars brought – Edith finds they give purpose to her very existence – the older

Electricity at Downton Abbey

Initially, Downton Abbey has electricity installed on the ground floor only, but by 1916 the family's bedrooms and the servants' quarters, both in the attics and below stairs, have been electrified. Electricity is not supplied from a mains source but has its own generator, which could require six engineers to run it. 'The men who operated the generator were very highly respected,' says Julian. 'No one understood their job – they had mystique.'

Allen Leech is Tom Branson

'The car I drive is a 1920 Renault and it is
an absolute nightmare with all the double
declutching. The owner drives it first, then
I get in and the gears start clunking. Once I
heard a massive clunk and I looked back and
a huge piece of metal had fallen out into the
road – he had to go back and get it. He'd
driven that car to France and back, so I blame
the owner for losing half the gearbox, not my
gear changing! It's a hand-crank start and you
have to be careful how you do it because once
it starts spinning you can lose your thumb.'

generations complained that house parties were forever changed. 'Until cars the hostesses were in control of when you arrived and when you left,' explains Julian. 'You would be told, "Please catch the 4.30 at Waterloo and then on Monday you will be put on the 3 o'clock." Suddenly the young were saying, "I'm sure we'll be there in time for dinner".' A hostess's carefully laid plans would also be disrupted when, for example, the guests would decide to get in the car and drive down to Brighton for the afternoon. London began to feel empty on a Saturday as society people rediscovered country houses as both a pleasant place to stay and the better place to be seen. Carriages were no longer taken to Hyde Park to parade; instead men and women piled into motor cars and drove off to the latest fashionable country house. It was the end of the rather more sedate Saturday-to-Monday tradition and the beginning of the 'weekend' as we would recognise it today.

The world of science was developing at such a rate that it captured the public imagination. Around the turn of the century, the socialist and novelist H.G. Wells reflected the mood of the time when he effectively began a new literary genre with his science-fiction novels *The Time Machine* and *The First Men in the Moon*. Although published in 1895 and 1901 respectively, these books remained popular for many years and were referenced frequently in conversations amongst readers, much as we might talk about a hit television show. 'I feel as if I were living in an H.G. Wells' novel,' says Violet, when she is affronted by the newly installed telephone.

Writers such as E.M. Forster, Rudyard Kipling and Sir Arthur Conan Doyle enjoyed large readerships for their books at this time – the latter two would have been read by Lord Grantham and his family, as well as their servants. Even so, 1914 saw Conan Doyle's last Sherlock Holmes novel, *The Valley of Fear*, published as a magazine serial: he had tried to kill the character off but public outrage forced him to bring back his popular detective. Bernard Shaw's play *Pygmalion*, about the transformation of a working-class flower girl into a Society lady, was first performed in London the same year. The play would have highly amused Violet, if only because she thought the premise far too absurd ever to ring true.

Bigger audiences were to be seen at music halls, the primary source of entertainment for the working classes, but by 1912 they had become such draws that the first Royal Command Performance of a variety show was held for King George V and his wife in London. Just a few hundred yards down the road, music-hall star Marie Lloyd staged her own, more

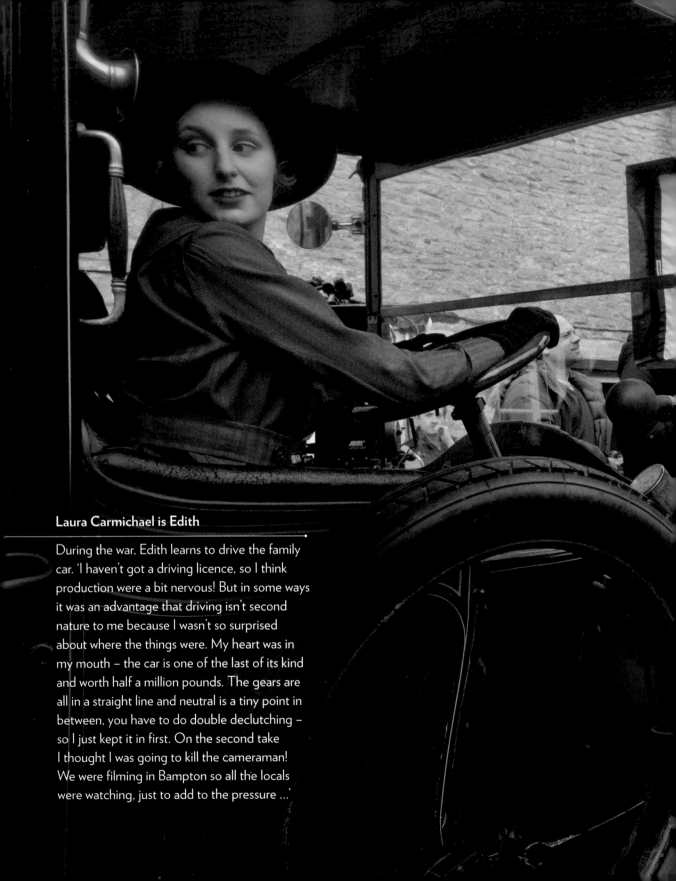

Laura Carmichael is Edith

During the war, Edith learns to drive the family car. 'I haven't got a driving licence, so I think production were a bit nervous! But in some ways it was an advantage that driving isn't second nature to me because I wasn't so surprised about where the things were. My heart was in my mouth – the car is one of the last of its kind and worth half a million pounds. The gears are all in a straight line and neutral is a tiny point in between, you have to do double declutching – so I just kept it in first. On the second take I thought I was going to kill the cameraman! We were filming in Bampton so all the locals were watching, just to add to the pressure ...'

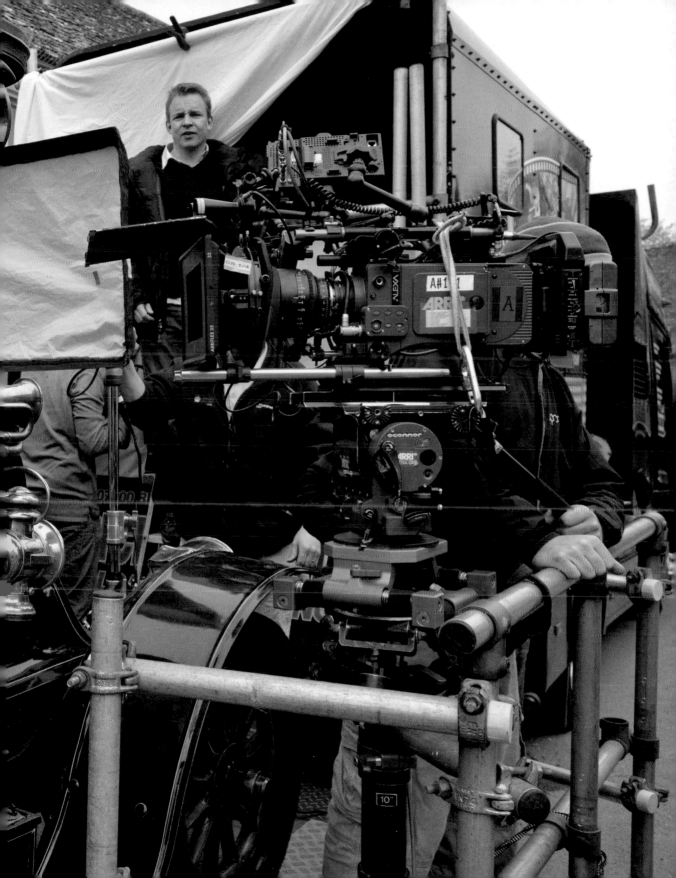

raucous, event: 'A Command Performance by Order of the British Public'. It was her revenge for having been left off the royal bill (her repertoire was considered too rude for the delicate ears of the king).

Technology, too, had helped promote these acts. Trains meant entertainers could travel all over the country to perform, tabloid newspapers meant their complicated private lives were entertaining fodder for the masses and the arrival of cheap, mass-produced pianos meant families could buy sheet-music to play the show songs at home – a kind of 'pop music' for the time. 'It's A Long Way To Tipperary', written by a composer and a semi-professional singer who ran a fish stall, was a sheet-music hit when it came out in 1912 and, two years later, towards the end of the first year of the war, was selling 10,000 copies every day.

VIOLET, THE DOWAGER COUNTESS
'The young are all so calm about change, aren't they?'

Moving pictures were a growing craze. From 1908 music halls had started to put screens into their theatres, a few even converting into cinemas. By 1911, Brighton had four cinemas, including the old roller-skating rink that had become The Grand Picture Palace. Hour-long films would show three times a week – mostly American movies but the British soon jumped onto the bandwagon. Epping Forest in Essex and Box Hill in Surrey were the unlikely locations for filming stories about cowboys and Indians. The cinemas were fuggy, smelly places, not least because everyone smoked cigars and cigarettes throughout the screening. Naturally enough, the war stopped productions and, thanks to a general shortage of money and enthusiasm to make them, it took until the mid-1920s for the film industry to recover.

Even the art world was changing, although most people were too set in their ways to embrace the new styles of painting. A daring exhibition was held by the art critic Roger Fry in November 1910, showing works by Pablo Picasso, Henri Matisse, Paul Cézanne, Paul Gauguin and Vincent van Gogh. Most thought he was insane. It was said that old ladies were carried out of the gallery after fainting in shock. Only one critic, Hugh Blaker, predicted that 'cultured London is composed of clowns who will by the

Early aviation

Even more exciting and extraordinary than the arrival of the motor car was the invention of air travel. The famous Wright brothers achieved the first motorised, sustained flights on 17 December 1903, climbing to 36m (120ft) in 12 seconds and 260m (852ft) in 59 seconds. Just a few years later, on 5 July 1911, an aeroplane flew over London for the first time. In April 1918 the Royal Air Force came into existence and fighter planes were a key part of wartime strategy. More happily, by 1919 there were commercial flights between London to Paris and in June of that year the first successful non-stop Transatlantic flight took place.

THE GREAT AIR RACE

SENSATIONAL DESCRIPTIVE FANTASIA FOR THE PIANOFORTE.

By LAWRENCE WRIGHT.

THE LAWRENCE WRIGHT MUSIC Co
8, DENMARK St. (Charing Cross Road)
LONDON W.C.

Agents for Australia and New Zealand, ALLAN & Co Proprietory Ltd, 276 - 278 Collins St MELBOURNE

way be thoroughly ashamed in twenty years' time and pay large sums to possess these things. How insular we are still.' Happily, he was proved right.

The brutality of the First World War had a revolutionary effect in its own right, forcing medical developments and aggressive warfare tactics, which meant tanks, poison gas and fighter planes were all deployed for the first time. The horrendous conditions experienced in the trenches and the huge numbers of wounded soldiers that came through the field hospitals meant that doctors had to be extremely innovative in finding ways to deal with injuries quickly and hygienically, often using minimal equipment. Ongoing research in sanitation, nutrition, surgery and chemistry all promoted effective new treatments. The safety of blood transfusions improved (although there was a shortage of donors) and drinking water could now be purified by liquid chlorine. Amputations were a last resort, with efforts being made to preserve limbs if possible.

To be injured in this war was horrific: pain could only be dulled with chloroform and morphia; there were no antibiotics and gangrene was an ever-present threat. The invention of poison gas was another terror. Although about 97 per cent of gassed soldiers survived, their evacuation and the treatment of their inflamed eyes and blistered skin meant the medical services found it hard to cope. The gas mask was invented just in time – 1914 – but it was not until two years later that an effective small box respirator was rolled out to the British Army, too late for many soldiers.

The rise of Socialism and the suffragette movement signalled some of the most far-reaching changes of the time. The voices of the working classes and women were at last being heard and the all-encompassing need to pull together to fight the war at home and abroad broke down many social barriers, some permanently. By 1919, David Lloyd George was Prime Minister, heading up a coalition government of Liberals and Conservatives. The First World War was over, but Spanish 'Flu was threatening to take as many lives as the battlefield had. Women over 30 and all men now had the vote; Lady Astor became the first female MP to take her seat in the House of Commons and the first female bar student was admitted to Lincoln's Inn. It was normal to travel by motor car, to commute to work, go on the London Underground, take the train cross-country, stay with friends for the weekend and see a movie at the cinema. You could also telephone someone, read a tabloid newspaper for tittle-tattle and drink a cup of instant coffee. Modern Britain was born.

Life in Service

CHAPTER FOUR

EXT. KITCHEN COURTYARD. DOWNTON. DAY.

At a table in the yard,
O'Brien is with Thomas;
he fiddles with a clock. He has oil
and screwdrivers and cloths. They are
both smoking surreptitiously.

'Brien and Thomas are snatching a few moments to themselves, sitting in the yard by the kitchens. Here they can indulge in a private habit or two – whether it's smoking or slouching with their hands in their pockets – but even now, in a break from their performance on what they have come to think of as the stage above stairs, they can never leave their roles far behind. We see them in uniform, a sort of costume that keeps them in character, as they prepare their props for their next scene.

Just like the backstage of a theatre, the below stairs quarters – the kitchen, servants' hall, butler's pantry and housekeeper's sitting room – are where the props are kept, all ready to be used on set at just a second's notice. Gleaming silver, pressed linens, polished crystal – these objects remind the family and their guests that they are watching a first-rate performance. Even the servants' uniforms are part of the show: the stiff collars, starched shirts, laced boots and tied-back hair help the actors to get into character from the moment they dress in the morning. The sombre colours and simple details emphasise the seriousness of the parts they play and as they climb the stairs the expressions on their faces change: impassive masks hide whatever they were feeling before they stepped out into the great hall. The arrogant curl of Thomas's lip, William's joking grin, the worried, furrowed brow of Carter – these vanish with a turn of the handle on the green baize door.

A hundred years ago, and before, a job in service was a desirable thing. For those born into the working classes it meant work that was secure and, perhaps more interestingly, it meant that you became a part

Jim Carter is Carson

'We were taught that we have tremendous pride in our work and we were not to feel over-deferential ... We don't have to bow and scrape – we are an integral part of keeping the house running smoothly.'

Rob James-Collier is Thomas

'I like the scenes below stairs because I have lines! Siobhan is a fantastic actress to work with – you really learn from her. She's very measured and it's all in the eyes. In rehearsal you think there's nothing going on and then you see it on screen and you think "wow – everything's happening".'

Julian Fellowes on O'Brien

'O'Brien realises that she is never going to be rich or successful – although she is quite successful as the lady's maid of a countess. But she gets her thrills by manipulating and being devious and plotting. Her reward is in having a sense that she has power over people.'

of a life that would otherwise remain completely out of reach. Of course, as a servant you could never become absolutely assimilated – you moved within the rooms of a grand house much as an actor would perform upon an elaborately decorated stage. You were an integral part of it and yet you could relax and be yourself only when back in the wings.

O'Brien moves almost seamlessly between floors; she is very good at her job, proud to be so, and her ease amongst both servants and family is a measure of this. Of all of the servants, O'Brien is probably the best actor, showing only the face she wants her colleagues or her employer to see. Lady Grantham, after all, believes they are friends.

O'BRIEN

'Friends? Who does she think she's fooling? We're not friends.'

The top jobs for a woman in service were housekeeper, cook and lady's maid. O'Brien, as lady's maid to a countess, is a woman with a career. This is no insignificant thing: to attain it meant the acquisition of skills, not to mention the sacrifice of a husband and children. Such high positions rarely allowed for marriage and a family, even though housekeepers and cooks were always known as 'Mrs'. Why O'Brien has remained unmarried is not revealed, but the fact that she has chosen to remain single is certainly to the advantage of her career progression.

What we do know of O'Brien is that she was born in the north of England as the daughter of a farmer. As such, she would have been following family tradition in choosing to enter service, both as a good means of employment and also to improve her marriage prospects. A bright girl, she may even have been selected from her classroom, along with two or three others, when the châtelaine from the local great house came down with her housekeeper to choose new maids. Every girl in that school would have been craning her neck and giving her brightest smile, hoping for a chance to gain a position that would relieve her from the tedium of work at the farm.

Going to work in a big house was cause for excitement; not only did it offer a young man or woman secure employment with the prospect of promotion, it also broadened their experience by introducing them to

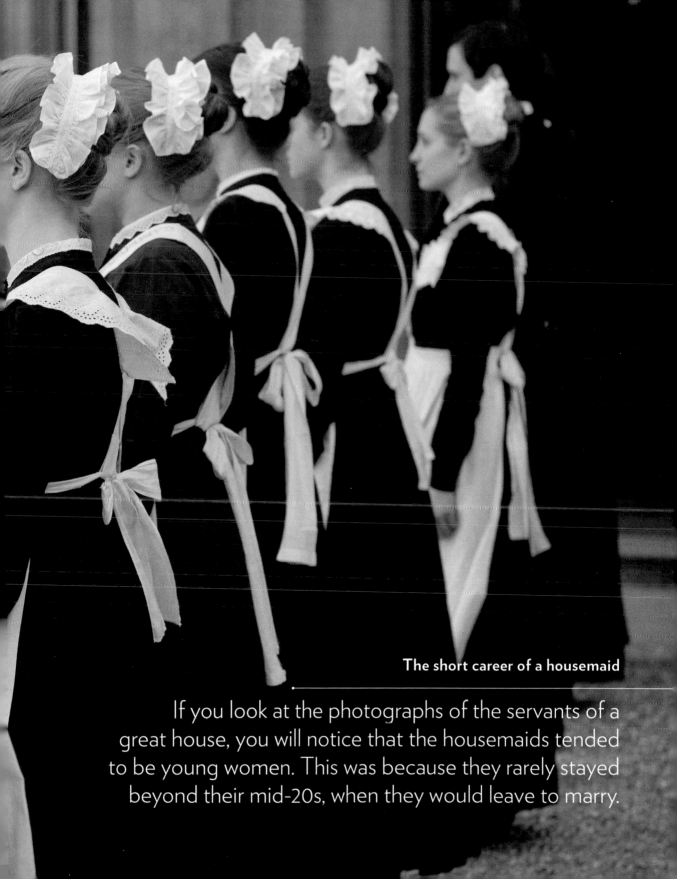

The short career of a housemaid

If you look at the photographs of the servants of a great house, you will notice that the housemaids tended to be young women. This was because they rarely stayed beyond their mid-20s, when they would leave to marry.

a different way of life. Work as a farmhand or shop girl may have meant more freedom in the evenings – and possibly more time off – but their family, probably already financially stretched to the limit, would have faced the burden of feeding, housing and clothing their offspring. Although the hours were long and the pay could be relatively stingy, work in service did provide clothing, in the shape of material for a uniform, three meals daily and a roof over their head. Not that this would have meant much in the way of comfort, as their private quarters would have been akin to a starving artist's garret.

Beginning her career in service as a housemaid, O'Brien would have been quick to see the merits of work as a lady's maid. With the right mistress, it could mean opportunities for travel, as well as for self-improvement. However, in order to attain the position she would need to learn how to dress hair, and possibly even speak some French. The ability to darn a few socks wouldn't quite cut it; a lady's maid had to know how to do invisible mending and be able to make her mistress's underwear. At a certain point, O'Brien would have decided to take her work seriously, perhaps saving up to put herself through a hairdressing course, so as to add it to her repertoire and make her a more attractive prospect to a future mistress. To say that you had been trained in Paris or were known for doing hair well could be a big recommendation; the great ladies invested in their lady's maids, often paying generous sums to employ someone who could make them look stylish.

CORA

'There's one I think has real possibilities. She learned to do hair in Paris, while she was working for the Ambassadress.'

This position was one of the few that meant you became truly intimate with the family, becoming privy to their secrets as you blended silently into the background in their bedrooms. As O'Brien turns both frustrated and embittered she uses her privileged knowledge as a means of asserting what little power she has, both above and below stairs. Despite all the perks, there is no getting away from the fact that having a top job in service restricted your freedom. At that level the servants were

The life of a lady's maid

Having learnt French in Ripon and completed two years' apprenticeship at a dressmaking establishment, Rosina Harrison got her first position as a lady's maid to a Miss Patricia, the 18-year-old daughter of Lady Ierne Tufton, in London, in 1917. 'As well as repairing clothes I made quite a lot of underlinen. Material would be sent from France and Miss Emms [Lady Ierne's lady's maid] and I would make it up into pants, slips, petticoats and vests. Underwear was very different in those days... Bust bodices, camisoles and petticoats were much more the vogue and corsets were worn from quite a young age – made and fitted personally, of course.'

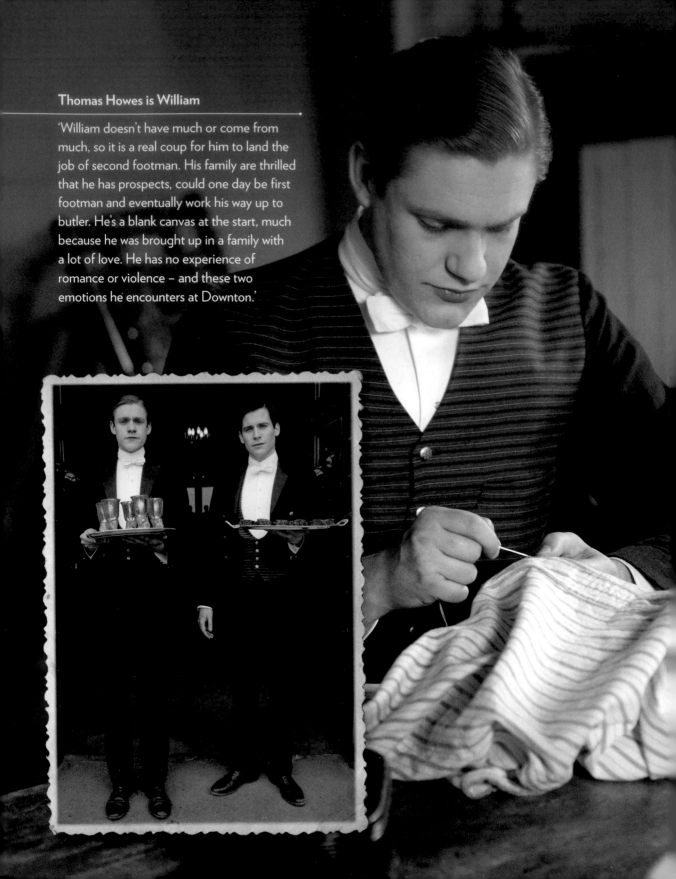

Thomas Howes is William

'William doesn't have much or come from much, so it is a real coup for him to land the job of second footman. His family are thrilled that he has prospects, could one day be first footman and eventually work his way up to butler. He's a blank canvas at the start, much because he was brought up in a family with a lot of love. He has no experience of romance or violence – and these two emotions he encounters at Downton.'

at the beck and call of their master and mistress from morning till night, seven days a week. Your time off might be as little as an afternoon – that is, a couple of hours – a week and every other Sunday.

Yet Carson, as one of the principal players in this production, enjoys his position and is only too delighted to fully embrace the family he works for as his own. He is perhaps rather like an actor who is unable to leave his character behind at work: even off-stage he feels he must maintain the mask of the dignified butler with a ramrod-straight back. Having to do or say anything that breaks away from the script always makes him feel deeply uncomfortable.

BATES TO WILLIAM

'He learned his business and so will you. Even Mr Carson wasn't born standing to attention.'

Some of the other servants are less sure of their role. William, the second footman, for example, is confused. On the one hand, he knows his job at Downton Abbey has given him the opportunity to better himself, and he has a reverential respect for the family he works for, but fundamentally he is just a nice local boy; someone who would be far more content mucking out a stable than standing in a grand hall balancing glasses on a silver tray. The fact that his parents burst with pride when he got the job means he can never contemplate leaving.

When he first started out, leaving home would have been a daunting prospect – as a boy of 13 or 14 years old, he would have had to say good-bye to his family, hardly knowing what lay ahead, amongst people he had never met before.

William would have had his first bite at the cherry as a lamp boy or hall boy at Downton Abbey, earning promotions as and when the positions became available. Reaching the post of second footman would have been cause for considerable celebration. Donning the elaborate livery for the first time would have been momentous: the clothes would have been tailored to fit him beautifully with stiffly starched shirt fronts that would square his shoulders, and his smart leather shoes would squeak as he quickened his step walking for miles around the house's halls and passages. The

Jim Carter is Carson

'Filming in two locations does keep your acting fresh. I haven't exactly got a low status above stairs but it is different, and then I have a very high status below stairs. I know my position when at Highclere Castle, shooting for two weeks, and then we go to Ealing Studios [the location for the servants' quarters] and it's a whole new set of things.'

THE BUTLER: A TRUSTED POSITION

Charles Dean, born in 1895, was second footman for the Duke of Beaufort, then under-butler with Edwin Lee for the Astors, before working as butler for Princess Obolensky, Nancy Astor's cousin by marriage.

'The thing about being a butler/valet is that you're in very close contact with the family. With the Obolenskys, whom I'd joined at the beginning of their marriage, I was able to watch happiness turn into mutual acceptance, lovers' tiffs turn into wrangling, boredom lead to suspicion; things were said that couldn't be taken back and consolation was sought from others who were more than ready to offer it.

'People are quick to criticise the morals of the rich and aristocratic, forgetting the temptations that are always there. Under stress and emotion employers sometimes forgot themselves and asked for opinions, and even advice, from their near servants.'

increase in pay would also have been worth celebrating: William's wage as second footman may compare to Gordon Grimmett's, who at the age of 18 in 1920 worked for the Astors in the same position. He earned £32 a year, with two shillings and sixpence a week extra for beer and washing money. This is the equivalent to about £700 a year in today's money, with a supplement of £5 a week, with full board and meals included.

While the wages of a house servant were not as good as those of a farmhand, miner or factory worker, they had no living expenses and their income would be boosted with tips from the family and guests. This bonus was not one enjoyed often by those servants who worked out of sight, but they could find other ways of supplementing their income, such as selling used corks, cook's grease, bits of clothing or rabbit skins.

Pride, too, would have compensated for a want in income. The servants at Downton Abbey work for the family of an earl, which in itself denotes that they are both good at their jobs and flourishing in their careers. Not just because they had probably escaped a life of rural hardship, but also because they were able to bask in the reflected glory of their employers' aristocratic status. It was vastly better as a servant to be working for the nobility than for a Mr and Mrs Suggs of Suburbsville: it elevated your social standing and improved your chances of future employment. It was the equivalent of playing for the bright lights of Broadway, rather than in fringe theatres.

However, changing venue was necessary if you wanted to be promoted into a better position or earn higher wages: if you decided to wait for the opening of butler, housekeeper or cook to come up in your house, you could still be waiting 20 years later. Deciding where to go was not too tricky; there was a 'servants' underground' which not only kept people informed of job opportunities in the bigger houses but also yielded information on what potential employers were like. If anyone treated their servants badly, they could find themselves short-handed pretty quickly, not to mention that a whisper of scandal could whip round the great estates of England faster than any telegram – as Mary discovered after the Kemal Pamuk affair.

CARSON

'I have received a letter, m'lady. From a friend of mine. He's valet to the Marquess of Flintshire.'

Lady's maid Rosina Harrison revealed, 'We had a "Who's Who" and a "What's What" below stairs, which contained more personal and colourful information about the gentry than ever the written version did. There was also a black list, and woe betide anyone who got on it. It could spell ruination for any hostess.'

Service

Before the First World War, 1.4 million people were employed as domestic servants. It was one of the largest single employment groups – just outnumbering agricultural workers and coal miners – and was largely made up of women. Around 15–20 per cent of this number would have been working in the houses of the nobility and the landed gentry.

Joanne Froggatt is Anna

'I really like the relationship with Lady Mary – it's an interesting friendship/professional relationship. They're about the same age and they're both young women embarking on life, but there's always that line between employee and servant.'

A butler's bond

Edwin Lee, the butler at Cliveden, could almost be said to have influenced the course of history, thanks to his close relationship with his employer, Nancy Astor (right). When Lady Astor's husband became a Viscount, his promising career as an MP ended, much to his fury, as he had to go and sit in the House of Lords. It was then suggested that perhaps she might stand to take his place. 'One day she sent for me. "Oh Lee," she said, "I've talked to so many people about Plymouth, what do you think I should do?" "I should go for it, my lady," I replied.

'Now I'm not so big-headed as to think that my opinion swayed her in any way but a couple of days later she again sent for me. "Lee, I've decided to take your advice. I'm going to 'go for it' as you said." She did, and it's now history that she was the first woman to take her seat in the House of Commons.'

However, a family had to behave honourably towards their servants, not just to ensure that they had enough staff serving at their dinners and receptions but also because they needed to be certain of their loyalty. Standing discreetly in the background, a servant would be almost forgotten while the family discussed their private concerns, or, as happened to Mary and Cora at the sudden death of Kemal Pamuk, they may even rely on their servants' assistance to help them conceal a private shame.

Of course, discretion couldn't always be relied upon. Juliet Nicolson, in her book *Perfect Summer*, writes that one man's butler admitted to him that the greatest amusement a servant could hope for was to piece together a torn-up letter, retrieved from an upstairs waste-paper basket. '"Far more entertaining than jigsaw puzzles," he confided.'

Such a bound-up connection does not mean, however, that the lines were not always clearly drawn. While the servants may have known a lot about the business of the family they worked for, most of their knowledge will have been learned by accidental overhearing, if not eavesdropping – they would rarely have been invited in to be told secrets.

ANNA

'What is the first law of service?
We do not discuss the business of this
house with strangers!'

By contrast, the family would know very little of their servants' private lives, to the degree that they would hardly even venture into the parts of the house that the servants occupied. This was in part because of the family's respect for their servants' boundaries, but they probably also assumed that there wouldn't be much of interest to them there. Families were as occupied by the soap opera of their own lives and those of their friends and acquaintances as their servants were. In other words, they would rather be listening and laughing to the principal actors on stage than feigning any interest in the backstage machinations.

But, naturally enough, the very proximity of the working relationship between master and servant, particularly a 'body servant' such as a valet or lady's maid, meant that a kind of friendship could grow, with the one asking advice of the other.

Joanne Froggatt is Anna

'Upstairs is definitely quieter than downstairs! There are a lot of us in the servants' hall and it can get rowdy. There are so many people that are so funny to work with that it gives a different feel to the scenes. It's like Brian Percival [the director of Series One] said, "a swan on the surface with the legs flapping wildly beneath". The scenes upstairs are calm, controlled, correct, and downstairs it's too busy for politeness – the pressure is heightened. We're beavering away downstairs, so when we go upstairs it's like putting your head above water.'

A strict order of precedence below stairs – some might say, stricter than the class divide above stairs – also determined matters. Carson the butler is at the top of the pecking order, followed closely by Mrs Hughes, the housekeeper. While the butler is uppermost in seniority, he would largely be concerned with the work of the male servants. The housekeeper would have the housemaids under her direct supervision. The cook was answerable to both housekeeper and butler, but was also mistress of her own domain entirely, managing the kitchen staff. As you can imagine, this was the cause of arguments in many a household. Furthermore, while there were, of course, cases of mistresses treating their servants badly, it was more usual to find that young maids and boys suffered exploitation and oppression at the hands of their direct bosses.

LORD GRANTHAM

'We all have different parts to play, Matthew. And we must all be allowed to play them.'

Nevertheless, slowly but surely at the beginning of the twentieth century, as social lines blurred and moved, a life in service began to lose its sheen of respectability. The pride that the older servant had in his or her work began to take a knock, as the younger generation preferred to choose careers in shops, factories or offices. With improving literacy and a wider access to popular culture, such as radio and the cinema, even those born and brought up in rural outposts began to see that modern life could offer them more options and adventures than it did for their parents. Then the war, with all the chaos and change that it brought with it, put the final seal on attitudes towards a life lived downstairs. Former footman Gordon Grimmett noticed that 'as a result of the First World War domestic service was considered inferior employment for both men and women'.

Bates is desperate to hold onto his job as valet as that world was unkind to disablement, especially before the First World War, but most valets could afford to see each position as a stage in their journey, not a career choice. Now that he has met Anna, he is probably even more glad of the work. O'Brien seems to have made a decision about her life's direction – one that means she is a career woman, rather than raising a

Brendan Coyle is Mr Bates

'Bates comes from a generation of men and
a time where we didn't have a confession
culture and didn't talk about how we felt.
Serving with Lord Grantham broke those
class barriers down, but Hugh and I didn't
specify what exactly brought that about.
We think we should keep the audience
guessing and we keep ourselves guessing.'

Sophie McShera is Daisy

'I don't think she's ambitious. She's just surviving.
She's doing her best not to get told off and get
through the next job or hour.'

GOING ON THE LLOYD GEORGE

The beginnings of the welfare state system were established by the then Chancellor of the Exchequer (later Prime Minister) David Lloyd George, particularly with the passing of his 1911 National Insurance Act, which meant that workers were covered in cases of sickness and invalidity. However, Lloyd George's provision of welfare was raised through taxes on alcohol, tobacco, incomes and land, which incensed land-owners. There was, as a result, an intense political divide between the working classes, represented by Lloyd George and the Liberal Party in the House of Commons and the aristocracy, represented in the House of Lords.

JOE

'But what'll happen when you retire?'

MRS HUGHES

'I should think I'll stay here.
They'll look after me.'

Many members of the upper classes were offended by the suggestion that they did not properly look after their servants – in fact, long-serving servants were often given either a pension or accommodation in an estate cottage by their employers on retirement. Others may have had saving schemes, whereby a part of the servants' income was retained by their employers, to earn interest. Of course, this only really applied to faithful service of many years – if you moved around (which was often necessary in order to gain promotions and pay rises) you would need to save carefully. Others continued to work into old age, and many seaside B&Bs and small hotels in the country were run by retired butlers newly married to a former housemaid.

Phyllis Logan is Mrs Hughes

'She's not lonely. She's got too much to do and is not a great one for reflecting on her past. She's quite content with her lot. She has nice quarters, she's in charge and she has respect. She'll probably croak it the minute she does retire.'

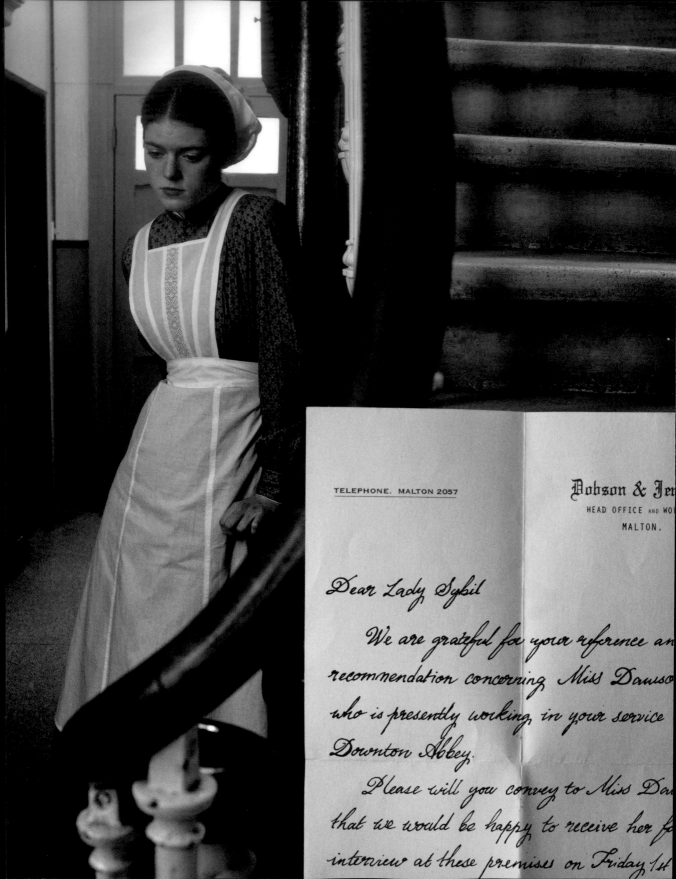

TELEPHONE. MALTON 2057

Dobson & Jen

HEAD OFFICE AND WO
MALTON.

Dear Lady Sybil

*We are grateful for your reference an
recommendation concerning Miss Dawso
who is presently working in your service
Downton Abbey.*

*Please will you convey to Miss Daw
that we would be happy to receive her fo
interview at these premises on Friday 1st*

family – but unlike Carson, who regards the family he works for as his own, she sits uncomfortably with her choice. While O'Brien takes pride in her skill and enjoys the friendships she has at Downton, she also derides her job as ridiculous.

The growing professional middle classes, people such as Matthew, who took a pride and interest in their work, increasingly could not fathom the desire of one person to serve another, particularly not when that work meant doing things for someone who could easily do it for themselves. However, even those aristocrats who did not believe they had a divine right to be served by others often felt their position carried with it an obligation to maintain a social and economic structure that had long been established. It was not theirs to change.

GWEN

'Who's been in my room? They had no right.'

MRS HUGHES

'See here … none of the rooms belong to you. … I am in charge of your welfare and that gives me every right.'

For housemaid Gwen, the lack of privacy, long working hours and the weight of traditional expectation has stirred in her a desire to change her life's direction. Her ambition to be a secretary may seem modest to us, but in 1913 the idea of a farmer's daughter giving up a good position in a house to take a chance on a business occupation would have seemed delusional. Fortunately, Gwen's steely determination and the support of Lady Sybil sees her out of the door of Downton into the brave new world.

In these modern times the lines are drawn differently, and while we all have parts to play, they are not as they were once written. Mostly the social progress and changes brought about are beneficial, but we must not patronise the people of a hundred years ago. They understood who and what they were – they were not divided into aristocratic snobs or servile beings. They were making the best of the world they were in and much of the time they were enjoying themselves as they did so.

Style

CHAPTER FIVE

Thomas is distracted by William,
who is about to go out with a serving dish.

Thomas: 'What do you look like?
Daisy, what do you think he looks like?'

Daisy hesitates.
This makes her uncomfortable.

Thomas: 'Do your buttons up.'

*T*homas's attack on William is prompted by nothing so much as an undone button or two, but for a footman, hired for good looks and height, his livery is the mark of status; to be shabby in appearance meant he would command no respect. From footman to duke, all items of clothing were carefully selected so that they would denote the wearer's position in society.

Clothes for family and servants alike did not just maketh the man but the entire structure of the day, and the outfit put on in the morning was seldom the one taken off last thing at night. Housemaids had different uniforms for the morning and afternoon, while footmen had one jacket for upstairs, another for down. Aristocratic men, too, had wardrobes of attire for formal, informal and special occasions, not to mention out-door sports and hunting, but it was the upper-class women who perhaps experienced both the best and the worst sensations that clothes could bring. The ladies wore fabrics of extraordinary richness in both feel and colour, trimmed with fine lace or soft, warm fur, or decorated with exquisite, delicate, hand-sewn embroidery. Haute couture was celebrated and innovations of design made the Edwardian period one of the prettiest and most colourful in years.

However, their enjoyment of the elaborate raiment was dampened slightly because of the practical difficulties attached to dressing and the number of times they had to get in and out of various clothes over the course of each day.

To begin at the beginning: the underwear. In the Dowager Countess's heyday, the most desirable shape for a woman was created by the 'S-bend'

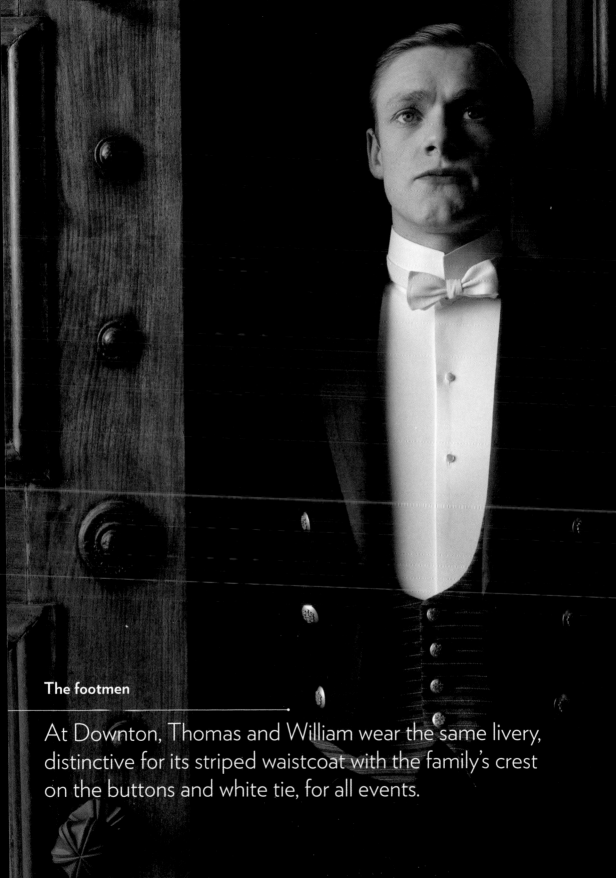

The footmen

At Downton, Thomas and William wear the same livery, distinctive for its striped waistcoat with the family's crest on the buttons and white tie, for all events.

THE COST OF
FASHIONABLE ENTERTAINING

Consuelo Vanderbilt, the American heiress who married the Duke of Marlborough, described a shooting weekend in 1896 which was in itself unexceptional, aside from the fact that they had the Prince and Princess of Wales staying. At the time the duchess was a young bride of 19 who found the whole experience exhausting, not just because she was in charge of all the pleasures of her guests (there were 30, which meant 100 people were in the house, including servants) but because of the munificence of clothes that went with it:

'The number of changes of costume was in itself a waste of precious time. To begin with, even breakfast, which was served at 9.30 in the dining-room, demanded an elegant costume of velvet or silk. Having seen the men off to their sport, the ladies spent the morning round the fire reading the papers and gossiping. We next changed into tweeds to join the guns for luncheon, which was served in the High Lodge or in a tent. Afterwards we usually accompanied the guns and watched a drive or two before returning home. An elaborate tea gown was donned for tea, after which we played cards or listened to a Viennese band or to the organ until time to dress for dinner, when again we adorned ourselves in satin, or brocade, with a great display of jewels. All these changes necessitated a tremendous outlay, since one was not supposed to wear the same gown twice. That meant 16 dresses for four days.'

Michelle Dockery is Mary

'There was one scene where I had a corset visible, so it was made for me. After we had filmed it, we removed all the details – flowers and ribbons – to make it a plain corset and then I could wear that as it was a perfect fit. I'm taller than most actresses, so most corsets tend to be too short in the body.'

corset, so-called because it would accentuate the bosom, squeeze the figure in at the waist and then push out at the back. Tightly constrained and further restricted by padded bustles and layer upon layer of petticoats, ladies wearing it were necessarily slow and dainty in their movements. By 1914, however, corsets were changing: Cora and her daughters favour the modern, high-waisted construction which is lightly boned and flexible but still does the job of straightening the silhouette.

SYBIL

*'Golly, my corset's tight.
Anna, when you've done that, would
you be an angel and loosen it a bit?'*

EDITH

'The start of the slippery slope.'

Corsets were designed to reach from the chest (where they flattened the bosom) to low down on the hip, ensuring the perfect shape for the fashion of the time. Mary's slim, boyish figure is just right for the styles of the period, but even so, she too wears one. In fact, there is not a female in the house who doesn't, regardless of their social standing; even Daisy, young and tiny, has to wear one. The corset is a tricky construction and needs an extra pair of hands to pull the laces tight to achieve the best support and look. The laces were adjusted to tighten or loosen the structure as needed, but once the corset had been 'set' to the preferred size, and therefore body shape, it could be simply fastened and unfastened using hooks at the front.

Cora, as a married woman, has breakfast in bed, and so she is spared one change in the morning and instead enjoys a rest for a couple more hours than her daughters. Before dressing for the day, Cora's leisurely bath gives her the chance to try out a new beauty cream bought from the department store Pontings, in London's Kensington High Street.

Once trussed up in their undergarments, Mary, Edith and Sybil select their dresses. 'A lady's morning dress should be simple and refined, and suited to the time of day,' wrote Lady Colin Campbell in her *Etiquette of*

Good Society (1893). 'Lace, unless of a thick description, is not worn with morning attire… Neither is much jewellery consistent; plain gold and silver ornaments are permissible, but never precious stones, except in rings.' Assisted by the head housemaid, Anna, the girls choose something appropriate for the day's activities, whether a tweed suit for a shooting lunch or a pretty summer dress for a garden party.

O'BRIEN

'Her ladyship wants the fawn skirt Lady Mary never wears. The seamstress is going to fit it to Lady Sybil but I can't find it.'

Mary and Sybil are fashion conscious, finding new ideas in popular magazines such as *Women's Weekly* and *The Lady*, which they would then suggest to their seamstress, Madame Swann. Clothes are made to last as long as possible, with swatches of fabric reused as panels, lace cut down to make collars or cuffs and ribbons tied around hats, necks or waists. In 1912, the dresses have high waists shown off by thin belts and narrow skirts which were hard to walk in. Over the remaining years of the decade, these became looser and hemlines began to rise. By 1916, they are six inches up from the ground; by 1918, eight inches. Edith's summer dress for the garden party, which saw the announcement of the outbreak of war, has a pretty long lace collar. Mary is often distinctly unimpressed by her younger sister's efforts, sneering at Edith once, saying 'If I ever wanted to attract a man I'd steer clear of those clothes and that hat'.

The right accessories need to be chosen, too. Gloves and a hat are obligatory; lace gloves for the summer, soft kid leather in the colder months. Mary's hat has been updated from the previous summer with new silk flowers sewn on. Edith's has simply been cleaned. If they were going out, say to a village fair or show, they might also select a delicate purse to hang from their wrist, not that it would contain much. The girls rarely carry more than a token amount of money – if they buy something in the local shops, it can be charged to the house account – and they do not wear any make-up. Once they are dressed, Anna fixes their hair. Until they leave the schoolroom, the daughters wear their hair down. In

Susannah Buxton, costume designer

'These three dresses demonstrate well the different ways in which we brought the costumes together for the show. Mary's dress was made for her, Edith's was hired – it was previously used in the Merchant–Ivory production of *Room With A View* – and Sybil's is an original Edwardian summer dress.'

MRS BEETON'S GOOD WASH FOR THE HAIR (1861)

Ingredients

1 pennyworth of borax, $\frac{1}{2}$ pint of olive oil, 1 pint of boiling water.

Mode

Pour the boiling water over the borax and oil; let it cool; then put the mixture into a bottle. Shake it before using, and apply it with a flannel. Camphor and borax, dissolved in boiling water and left to cool, make a very good wash for the hair; as also does rosemary water mixed with a little borax. After using any of these washes, when the hair becomes thoroughly dry a little pomatum or oil should be rubbed in, to make it smooth and glossy.

just one day, when their presence in the schoolroom came to an end, the girls' hair went up and their hemlines went down. Of course, this means they can no longer just brush their hair and pin a small decoration on it; a more complicated chignon requires help from Anna. Mary also wants to try out the Marcel wave machine – an exciting invention that uses hot irons to curl her hair. These finer details of their appearance will be much easier to achieve when eventually, as married women, they have their own ladies' maids trained in dressing hair, instead of having to share the ministrations of the housemaid with their sisters.

Meanwhile, Robert is dressed by Bates. Not that he requires help getting into his trousers exactly, but one of Bates' duties is to select and iron his master's suit, starch the collar and choose the correct tie and cufflinks for the day's events. All of these elements would have to be absolutely right for the occasion. As Lady Colin Campbell's etiquette guide decreed: 'When it is said that a tweed suit is worn in the country, it must not be supposed that that costume is there suitable for every occasion and at all times of day... it is not considered good taste for a man to wear much jewellery. A plain, handsome ring, studs and sleeve-links, a watch-chain without pendants, will always look more seemly than a great display of elaborate ornaments.' In the new emerging society, upwardly mobile men like Sir Richard Carlisle would use their clothes to demonstrate their cash-rich status, by wearing expensive fabrics cut by the best tailors in town.

Susannah Buxton, costume designer

'This outfit was made for Maggie Smith as Violet. The fabric was created by reproducing an Edwardian print onto silk. The design was based on a jacket from the era. We used original lace for the edging and cuff detail. The blouse had a lace bow and high neck added. The hat has vintage cotton baubles covered with a fine net dyed to match the suit.'

Violet's dress is not fashionable but is entirely suited to her. Although she is still bound in by the punishing S-bend corset, it does at least help carry the dreadful weight of her skirts. The lace cuffs and high-necked collar would have been deemed just right for a woman *d'un certain âge*. The cane is not so much a walking aid as an instrument to emphasise her point (Violet is always making a point) with a sharp tap on the floor.

SYBIL

'I don't know why we bother with corsets? Men dont wear them and they look perfectly normal.'

Should the girls decide to go for a walk, they would need to change into a different outfit, a light woollen tweed suit and sturdier boots – but on simpler days, such as for the garden party, they make mercifully few changes. Cora, like many married ladies in her position, takes the opportunity on quiet afternoons to take off her corset and wear a teagown for an hour or two before getting into her evening dress. Its huge advantage was that it was always ornately decorated but simply cut, meaning it was the only garment a woman could conceivably get in and out of alone, as it could be worn without a corset underneath. Worn between five and seven o'clock, it gave rise to the French phrase '*cinq à sept*'. This referred to the hours when lovers were received, the only time of day when a maid wouldn't need to be there to help you undress and therefore discover your secret. Lady Colin Campbell's divorce had hinged on the fact that her clothes had clearly been fastened by a man who didn't know what he was doing; when her lady's maid saw her for her next change, the fastenings were higgledy-piggledy. But for Cora, the teagown is not for any illicit behaviour, just for respite from her underpinnings.

The evening is where the finery of the era really came into its own. Every night, even when the family is sitting down to dinner without any guests, they will have changed into evening dress. This means not just the formal white tie attire for the men – tails, starched shirt front, white bow tie – but full-length evening dresses, gloves and tiaras for the married women. 'For these families, white tie was worn for dinner until the Second World War,' says Julian Fellowes. 'Black tie began to be worn after around 1918 and even then it would only be during a men-only club

Susannah Buxton, costume designer

'I found a long strip of original fabric set on gold net, which was so fragile it had started to split, and used that for the top and sleeves. The blue peacock bodice came from Alfie's Antiques market. The beaded belt was found at a vintage fair and the blue silk chiffon used for the trousers came from Shepherd's Bush Market. The headpiece is an original, hired for the scene.'

dinner. The Duke of Rutland's brother-in-law once asked him if he ever wore black tie and he said, "Only if I'm dining alone with the duchess in her bedroom." He was a rather stuffy and senior peer, but nevertheless for the upper classes, black tie was very (to some uncomfortably) informal.'

Mary has several evening dresses to choose from. Deep reds and dusky pinks suit her pale skin and she wears them often. In the evenings, long gloves are worn and, in keeping with her youthfulness, her jewellery is kept simple. By 1916, the waists are lower and the skirts, accommodating the new length, are more of a tulip shape, allowing for more freedom in their movements. Men's fashion remained little altered.

'*Is there anything more thrilling than a new frock?*'

It is Sybil, of course, who is the most forward thinking with her wardrobe. Her trousers took their inspiration from the Ballet Russes, which came to London in June 1911 and caused a sensation with their daring colours and revealing costume. The designer Léon Bakst and ballet impresario Sergei Diaghilev influenced designers such as Paul Poiret, the 'Sultan of Fashion', who brought out collections with bright colours, oriental jupe-culottes, 'lampshade' tunics and decorated turbans. Poiret trained at the House of Worth and was famous for making trousers for women, which were considered a liberation; ironically he also designed the hobble skirt, which severely restricted their walk.

When she arrives downstairs for dinner in her blue outfit, Sybil's intention is to shock – and she certainly succeeds. No woman of her class, before Poiret's harem look, had ever been seen in trousers. Aside from those worn below their skirts by female miners in Wigan, trousers were an exclusively male garment in Britain. The message was clear: nothing that men did was off-limits to women, as far as Sybil was concerned. It was as strong a statement as the suffragettes' window-smashing and equally designed to shake the older generation out of their sensibilities. It isn't long before Sybil's lead is followed, albeit more for practicality than fashion, when Edith wears jodphur-style trousers to work on the farm during the war. By the 1920s, Chanel had introduced a sporting,

HUNTING

Every sport in the country brought with it another set of clothes – none more glamorously so, perhaps, than hunting. Women wore only black or blue for hunting, never the scarlet jackets that male members of the hunt sported, but Mary still looks elegant in a top hat with veiling so fine it is almost falling apart, and a long black jacket that has a split up the back to enable her to move freely while riding. Under the skirt she wears jodphurs to protect her legs while riding. The high, white cravat is called a 'stock', and the one worn here is an original from the period. Mary's jacket is made from twill, a tough wool which will protect her from thorns and in the event of a fall, and which is cut so close and tight that it actually helps keep her back steady and straight when galloping across the fields. She also dons leather

gloves and proper riding boots to protect her extremities. Ladies on horseback were still required to wear a corset underneath their riding attire, although it was shorter than those worn with dresses.

Rather less charming is the description by Ernest King on how he cleaned his master's hunting clothes: 'From horse and rider perspiring, from a fall in a muddy ditch or field, they can come back in a pretty mess, especially the coat tails. When in this state we would ask the housemaid to save us the contents of the chamber pots, at least a bucketful. It was truly miraculous in getting the dirt out. That was immediately followed, I hasten to add, by brushing with clean water. I've often wondered if all the smart and fashionable hunting folk ever knew of the means taken to keep their coats so smartly turned out.'

Dan Stevens is Matthew Crawley

'The formal wear is really uncomfortable with razor-sharp collars. You are forced to sit very straight because the shirts are so starched. Subtle things are different such as the way you put in cufflinks – the modern way is to pinch the cuffs, but that only began in the 1920s. Before that you would push them through from the middle.'

Susannah Buxton, costume designer

'Robert's white tie has been made by Savile Row tailors Huntsman, following an original design and taking four fittings from start to finish. It is the cut that makes it of that time, predominantly the shoulders, which are rounder and softer than today's. There are no synthetics in the fabric and everything is hand-sewn. He wears a tail coat, a white piqué waistcoat with pearl buttons, black trousers with a satin stripe down the sides and patent pumps. The starched shirtfront is buttoned onto the top of his trousers to stop it buckling.'

Michelle Dockery is Mary

'A lot of Mary's clothes were made, a few were originals. Susannah [costume designer] has such a nice eye. She keeps it simple and never likes to overload us with too much jewellery. The dress is the thing.'

trousered look for women to much acclaim, although it still took until after the Second World War for them to become widely accepted.

The focal point of Cora's evening dress is her jewels. These would be a mixture of wedding presents and gifts from her mother, but principally they would form part of the Grantham collection. Gems would be worn on her hands, at her throat and, in the evenings, in her hair with a light tiara or diamond stars. Elaborate family tiaras would appear at especially grand dinners but, although beautiful, they could weigh heavily upon the head, as Consuelo Vanderbilt discovered. When she married, her new husband spent a great deal of her father's money on replenishing the Blenheim collection, which had been severely depleted by his improvident forebears: 'Marlborough's ideas about jewels were equally princely, and since there appeared to be no family heirlooms, jewels became a necessary addition to my trousseau. It was then the fashion to wear dog-collars; mine was of pearls and had nineteen rows, with high diamond clasps which rasped my neck. My mother had given me all the pearls she had received from my father. There were two fine rows which had once belonged to Catherine of Russia and to the Empress Eugenie, and also a sautoir which I could clasp round my waist. A diamond tiara capped with pearl-shaped stones was my father's gift to me, and from Marlborough came a diamond belt. They were beautiful indeed, but jewels never gave me pleasure and my heavy tiara invariably produced a violent headache, my dog-collar a chafed neck. Thus bejewelled and bedecked I was deemed worthy to meet English society.'

In contrast to above stairs, servants' clothing was one area of their lives that was relatively straightforward. The maids had to make their own uniforms of two dresses: a print dress with a plain apron for cleaning in the morning, changing into a black dress with a more decorative pinny for the afternoons and evenings. This could be expensive: in 1890 the price of the fabric could eat up six months' of a scullery maid's wages. In many houses, a bolt of cloth was given to the maids at Christmas so they had only the work, but not the cost, of the dress. With just two uniforms, a maid couldn't wash them every day, and when she did launder them she would need to get them cleaned, dried and ironed overnight.

Bates would dress similarly to his master, the giveaway being only the lesser quality of the fabric used for his clothes. His collars would be just as stiffly starched, even if they are turned down – it was not until the 1920s that gentlemen wore soft collars. Because he has no duties in the

Whitaker Yates 13 BISHOPBRID
LONDON

Susannah Buxton, costume designer

'This dress (above) was made of original beading so delicate that it couldn't be worn again. The red dress (right) is made from a turn-of-the-century Spanish evening dress. We sourced beautiful silk chiffon and had it pleated for the cap sleeves and bands across the front. We built layers for the final effect, with embroidered lace laid over the deep-red satin under-dress. We used evening gloves from the costume house selection, which are "dipped down" – that is, run through with dyes to take the brightness out of the fabric.'

THE HOUSE OF WORTH

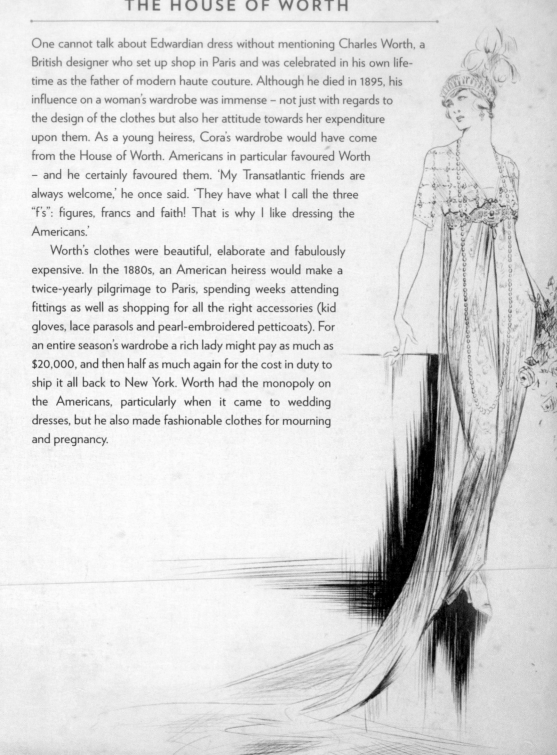

One cannot talk about Edwardian dress without mentioning Charles Worth, a British designer who set up shop in Paris and was celebrated in his own lifetime as the father of modern haute couture. Although he died in 1895, his influence on a woman's wardrobe was immense – not just with regards to the design of the clothes but also her attitude towards her expenditure upon them. As a young heiress, Cora's wardrobe would have come from the House of Worth. Americans in particular favoured Worth – and he certainly favoured them. 'My Transatlantic friends are always welcome,' he once said. 'They have what I call the three "f's": figures, francs and faith! That is why I like dressing the Americans.'

Worth's clothes were beautiful, elaborate and fabulously expensive. In the 1880s, an American heiress would make a twice-yearly pilgrimage to Paris, spending weeks attending fittings as well as shopping for all the right accessories (kid gloves, lace parasols and pearl-embroidered petticoats). For an entire season's wardrobe a rich lady might pay as much as $20,000, and then half as much again for the cost in duty to ship it all back to New York. Worth had the monopoly on the Americans, particularly when it came to wedding dresses, but he also made fashionable clothes for mourning and pregnancy.

Lesley Nicol is Mrs Patmore

'I know it doesn't look as if I've got a corset on, but I have! It is a challenge to wear. At the end of the day you'll see a lot of the female actresses bent over the kitchen table. It's the traditional method to relieve the corset – you lie face down with your body flat on the table and it takes the strain off the back. As well as the corset I wear an underskirt, petticoat, blouse, skirt, apron and the all-important little hat – I love that hat.'

evening, we never see Bates in a tailcoat. During the day, Carson, as was the tradition for butlers, wears a morning suit with a dark tie (tied with an old-fashioned knot because it's what he would have worn for years), but in the evening he could be mistaken for a gentleman in his white tie.

CARSON

'William, are you are aware the seam at your shoulder is coming apart?'

WILLIAM

'I felt it go a bit earlier. I'll mend it when we turn in.'

CARSON

'You will mend it now and you will never again appear in public in a similar state of undress.'

The real showpieces of the house were the footmen. Their uniforms would be provided by the house at great expense; when the men were offered the job, they would be told to go to the tailors to be fitted for the livery, trimmed with the family's crested buttons, and the cost would be charged to the family's account. At Downton, Thomas and William wear this uniform upstairs, but when they go through the green baize door into the servants' areas, they immediately hang up their tails so as not to spoil them and wear a 'downstairs jacket', which protects their white shirts. Even Thomas does this. He may be a servant but it's the crisp appearance of his livery that puts the arrogant curl on his upper lip.

Both before and during the First World War, the clothes worn by the family and servants alike were a clear indicator of status and position, and it would take more than the changes that had begun to occur within society during those war-torn years to change these habits.

Jessica Brown-Findlay is Sybil

'The best thing we found out was that by 1916 the stiff collars that nurses had had went out of use, as they just weren't practical – so I've got a soft collar, which is a relief. There's a grey underdress, which is plain and quite long. Pointed shoes, white cuffs, apron and a red cross on the sleeve. The headdress is quite severe – the hair and make-up department have a job trying to find a way for me to have a little fringe or curl at the side.'

WARTIME CLOTHING

For the most part, clothes did not change hugely during the war. Hemlines rose and there was a certain loosening of stays after the Air Board commandeered the supplies of steel used for the eyelets, as well as requisitioning the machines that made them. It was considered 'bad form' to wear evening dress to the theatre, but otherwise things remained more or less the same, except in two key places: those fighting on the home front and those serving in the fields.

Edith, working on a farm during the war, feels an immense liberation in wearing trousers. She has jodhpurs, last year's jacket relegated from best to 'working', overalls and knee-length boots. Most importantly, she has freedom in the way she walks and can now sit in a more casual way than she has ever been able to before.

Sybil, as a nurse, acquires a uniform. These were deeply practical if not always entirely attractive. Lady Diana Manners did not like hers at all: 'There was no long glass, but I later saw what was making my mother so appalled, for indeed I did look horrible. The dress was just off the floor and gathered at the back only. The print was of a minute and colourless mauve-and-white pin-stripe. The apron was cut to deform the figure. The stiff collar, cuffs, and belt gleaming with starch gave cleanth and trimness. The absurd cap attached to the tip-top of the head by an unreliable pin protected one's hair from neither lice nor from contagious germs. There were the universal black stockings and flat black shoes.'

FIVE THOUSAND BY JUNE

GRADUATE NURSES
YOUR COUNTRY NEEDS YOU

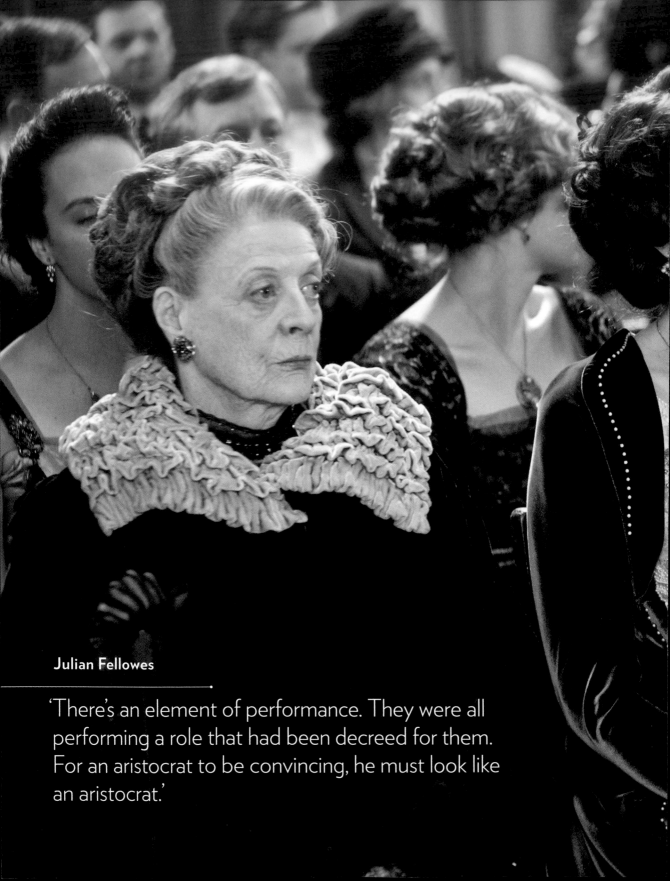

Julian Fellowes

'There's an element of performance. They were all performing a role that had been decreed for them. For an aristocrat to be convincing, he must look like an aristocrat.'

Rosalind Ebbutt, costume designer

'Regiments were invented for the series. Lord Grantham is with the North Riding Volunteers and Matthew is with the Duke of Manchester's Own. For each we had drawings done of their crests by the College of Arms and a specialist then made moulds of the artwork for their regimental badges.'

Uniform

Matthew, as an officer, would have his uniform made by his own tailor. In full dress he wears a shirt with a soft collar and tie, breeches, a service tunic that has buttons embossed with his cavalry regiment crest, field boots with laces and a Sam Browne belt, which is worn across the chest and around the waist. If a soldier was fighting in the trenches, he might wear puttees instead of his long boots – these were leg bindings worn over ankle boots, which made it easier to run around and also meant you saved your leather boots from being ruined in the mud. As the war progressed, officers stopped wearing their ranking badges because they made them too easy a target for the Germans. But so they could still be identified they designed battlefield emblems – colour swatches that would be sewn onto the back of their jackets. Other ranks wore tunics of much hairier fabric, with collarless grey serge shirts and tunics that buttoned up to the neck.

Mess kit

Lord Grantham's mess kit is copied from one that was worn by an officer in the Indian Guides in 1912. The fabric came from a firm in Yorkshire that specialises in making uniforms.

House & Estate

CHAPTER SIX

A door opens. Robert, 7th Earl of Grantham, walks out of his dressing room. With a growl of delight, Pharaoh bounds over to bid his master good morning, and to follow him. Robert is handsome and clever, but his life isn't as uncomplicated as one might think. He walks along the gallery and on down the massive staircase into the great hall. Now we see it in all its glory. This could only be the palace of an English nobleman.

When Robert walks down the stairs to breakfast each morning, he treads a well-worn path. Six former Earls of Grantham have walked before him – the house was bought by the Crawleys in 1679 – and Robert himself ran up and down those stairs as a small boy. He was born at Downton Abbey; he hopes he will die there, too. The very bricks of the building are as much a part of him as his own skin. For the house to belong to anybody other than an Earl of Grantham is inconceivable to him; if he did not pass it on to the next earl, he would not only feel that his entire life's work had been for nothing, but also that he had betrayed his predecessors, each of whom had managed to entrust it to the next generation.

Downton Abbey is more than a house, it is a whole civilization. For more than two hundred years the house and its estate would have provided employment and a way of life for many diverse people. As Julian Fellowes says: 'The family are not just the employers but the excuse.'

Looking after Downton Abbey is a full-time job for a large number of people. At the head of these, of course, is the Earl of Grantham himself. Since childhood it would have been constantly impressed upon him that his greatest duty is to the estate. There would never have been any question of him doing anything else or living anywhere else. In fact, when the future of the estate was under threat – thanks to the agricultural depression of the 1870s – Robert (then Viscount Downton) knew that his duty to his ancestral home meant that he must marry for money. Cora, an American heiress, seemed the perfect solution.

THE EARL OF GRANTHAM

'I have given my life to Downton. I was born here and I hope to die here. I can claim no career beyond the nurture of this house and this estate. It is my third parent and my fourth child. Do I care about it? Yes. I do care!'

Hugh Bonneville is Lord Grantham

'He [Lord Grantham] seems to step back when his daughter's inheritance is at stake. I talked to Julian Fellowes and Alastair Bruce about that concern ... it's the house and the estate that matters. That concept took some readjusting to, because surely one would want to do what was best for one's daughter. But there's more to it than that; for the Earl there's a whole community at stake.'

While there were not many 'arranged' marriages at this time, compared to the eighteenth century, there were some notable weddings that occurred because an aristocrat had an estate in need of the injection of cash which an American heiress (or any heiress, for that matter) could bring. Nobody was under any illusion that these were love matches, except for a few rare cases. 'Some of them were happy – the Duke and Duchess of Roxburghe, for example,' says Julian Fellowes. 'She arrived as the property millionairess of Manhattan and saved the house. It's now one of our best dukedoms and they were very, very happy. She embraced the life, she loved it and she loved her children – there's no sad story. But the Duke and Duchess of Marlborough and the Duke and Duchess of Manchester were miserable. There was an element of lottery.'

Luckily for Robert and Cora, they won the gamble and fell in love with each other not long into their marriage. 'Robert is a man who in his youth allowed himself to be entirely consumed with the need to keep the show on the road and so got pushed into this marriage,' says Julian. 'As he has come to know himself he has become nicer. He's okay because he fell in love with his wife, but he knows that he married her for her money and he is ashamed of the fact and it lingers with him still. He feels he can only justify himself if he takes the position seriously, and the responsibilities that go with it. That's not to say he doesn't enjoy his position – he's not a man in anguish – but he feels it is necessary to acquit himself of his duties first. So he disapproves when his daughters attempt to shrug off their responsibilities.'

He and Cora failed to produce 'an heir and a spare', and much as they love their three daughters, this did of course mean that he would have to pass on the estate to a man who was not his child. Lord Grantham liked his cousin's son, Patrick, and he was very much in favour of Mary marrying him – it would have kept matters very neat, to his mind. Patrick's death on the sinking *Titanic* was a tragic event, but Robert was happy to welcome Matthew Crawley, the next heir in line, growing to love him as they got to know each other. 'Matthew is his long-lost son,' explains Julian. 'In a way, he's had a soft landing because he will leave everything to someone he loves.'

But until the moment Matthew takes over, the estate at Downton is still in Lord Grantham's charge. Lord Grantham's, that is, and Carson's – whom Robert trusts with the day-to-day running of the house and managing the staff. For, strange as it might seem, when it came to the organisation of the house, the butler took care of much of the detail. The mistress of the house might choose the menus or draw up the guest lists or organise charitable events, but when it came to decisions on household business, she was entrusted with very little.

The master of the estate, on the other hand, could defer to the butler. According to Julian, this too is true at Downton: 'Robert believes, quite rightly, that he can't fight Carson if he feels strongly enough because he's the one running the house. That's the strange thing about the balance of power between them.' When it came to the hiring and firing of the staff, the housekeeper was in charge of the maids, but the butler was over and above that and when he had an opinion the master had to have a pretty good reason for not adhering to it – which was why Lord Grantham nearly lost the fight over Bates.

LORD GRANTHAM

'Don't worry, Carson. I know all about hard decisions when it comes to the honour of Downton.'

'I think one has to remember that in a life like this, the only other grown man he could talk to was the butler. You could talk to the valet, but you would be nervous because he was one of the servants. The butler was not one of the servants – he was a law unto himself,' Julian reveals. 'A secret with him would probably stay a secret.'

Besides Carson, there is, of course, the full complement of indoor staff, with whom we are familiar, but there is also a huge number of less visible, but just as important, staff working outdoors on the estate. This group includes a gamekeeper, in charge of the woodland and shooting; the head gardener, responsible for providing flowers inside the house – anything from a buttonhole to a funeral wreath and centrepieces – as well as cultivating the gardens themselves with the help of as many as 40 gardeners; the head coachman and perhaps ten grooms, if not more. At the turn of the century, as motor cars were produced in greater numbers and so became more widely available, the coachmen and grooms were slowly supplanted – albeit not entirely – by chauffeurs, which led to a

Hugh Bonneville is Lord Grantham

[Of himself and Carson] 'I'm the daddy of the upstairs and he's the daddy of downstairs. We both have a sort of benign dictatorship over our realms.'

Cliveden

A house similar in size to Downton Abbey, Cliveden had a staff of 12 working in the dairy. The estate owners, the Astors, even took one of their cows with them when they holidayed at their homes at Sandwich, in Kent, and Jura, in Scotland.

great deal of tension between them. Other staff would disparagingly call the chauffeurs 'shuvvers' and on seeing them would hook their thumbs into the armholes of their waistcoats, to signal their contempt. Some may have deserved it; shuvvers were inclined to think of themselves as gifted artisans, not servants, and could be arrogant. In addition, at Downton there are men to work the electricity plant, to act as telephone operators and even night watchmen. Given the constant work that needs to be done to maintain such a great house, there is also a wide range of odd job men around the estate, both permanently employed and brought in from the locality as and when they are needed; carpenters, plumbers and glaziers would also have been on the payroll.

LORD GRANTHAM

'*I'm meeting Cripps at five. I'll see you at dinner.*'

Downton Abbey, like many sizeable estates, has a 'home farm' that supplies the house with vegetables and meat, as well as a dairy which produced the milk, butter and cheese for the kitchen. Farming then was hugely labour intensive, with a lot of scything still done by hand, and substantial numbers of men required to work alongside the horse-drawn ploughs Gathering in the harvest was a slow process that took place over long, hard hours in the hot summer months. Tractors were just starting to be used, although whether the heavy, unwieldy machinery lightened the workload was questionable. Even so, when Edith turns her hand to farming during the war – as many women did – driving the tractor was one of her favourite jobs.

But while the surrounding landscape is impressive, it is the house that is most captivating. The grandeur of the great hall alone ensures any visitor is left in no doubt as to the splendour both of the house itself and the family's long and noble history. Unlike many of the families today who live in large estates and who cannot afford to heat every room or have given over parts of the house to paying residents, the Edwardians did not confine themselves to living in just two or three rooms but spread themselves out over the house.

The interiors of Downton in Robert's day are not fashionable; the most recent mistresses of the house, Violet, the Dowager Countess, and Cora, are not as concerned with picking up on the latest trends from Paris or London for the house as they are for their wardrobes. Like the Georgians and Victorians before them, the Edwardians knocked down walls and built on wings, changed round the front and back of the house and moved entire panelled rooms. They altered utterly the way in which these house were lived in; the introduction of electricity changed the way a room was lit and made an enormous difference to the look and atmosphere of the space. Such changes were not always greeted with approval. Violet is most displeased when Robert has electric light installed on the ground floor, commenting, 'Such a glare. I feel as if I were on stage at the Gaiety.'

LORD GRANTHAM

'I am a custodian, not an owner.'

Perhaps surprisingly, the majority of the rooms of the house are warm. We tend to think of country houses as being freezing cold. (Julian recalls staying in a house so icy that during the night he resorted to pulling more or less everything in the room bar the wardrobe – but including the bathroom towels and a large rug – onto his bed in an effort to stave off hypothermia.) However, in Edwardian times fuel prices were not an issue, and with plenty of fires lit and efficient plumbing for hot water, the rooms of the house would have been positively aglow with heat.

Although the décor does not reflect the latest interior trends, the details within the house would nonetheless impress a visitor. Indoor palm trees were in vogue, and huge pots of them draw the eye in the hall and drawing room at Downton. Great vases of flowers from the gardens are constantly replenished, as well as elaborate centrepieces for the dining table, and stags' antlers, bagged on hunts in Scotland, line the walls.

The fine features of the house are looked after with great care; the wood, marble and brass are carefully polished, sofas and chairs are re-stuffed regularly, rugs are beaten and the carriage clocks are properly maintained by Thomas, whose father was a clockmaker. With such care and attention, it is no surprise that everything lasts so long.

Continuity

Scenes involving food at Downton provided challenges for continuity. Dishes seen to be taken out of the kitchens, filmed at Ealing Studios, would appear again sometimes two weeks later when the footmen carried it into the dining room, filmed at Highclere Castle.

Most importantly, the peerage's mania for collecting meant that a house like Downton would have on display paintings, sculptures and tapestries of enormous historical significance and beauty. The colour of the walls mattered only in as much as they needed to set off these collections and show them at their best. There are great works by artists ancient, medieval and modern, as well as a near-constant commission of portraits from contemporary artists of note – John Singer Sargent being the most famous at this particular time. Many outstanding collections remain in houses today. Goodwood House, for example, the home of the Dukes of Richmond and Gordon for more than 300 years, has paintings by Van Dyck, Canaletto, Stubbs and Reynolds.

Up the grand stairs are numerous bedrooms for the family and visitors. To prevent any embarrassing mistakes, some houses would write the names of the guests on pieces of card and slip them into brass holders on the relevant bedroom doors. Lord Charles Beresford said that on one occasion he tiptoed into a dark room and jumped into a vast bed, shouting 'Cock-a-doodle-doo', only to find himself between the Bishop of Chester and his wife.

In each of the bedrooms, thick curtains are swagged at the windows, floors are laid with Persian rugs and there's a fresh posy of flowers (also cultivated by the head gardener) by the bed. Sprung mattresses are made up with crisp linen sheets, thick woollen blankets and a heavy bedspread smoothed over the top. At Downton there is a 'bachelors' corridor' of rooms in one part of the house, intended to keep any single male guests away from the daughters of the house (not that this was entirely preventable, as Mary learned to her cost). Married couples in the upper classes tended to sleep in separate bedrooms, although the affectionate Robert and Cora notably shun this practice.

The servants' quarters are contained in the basement and attics of this house. The bedrooms are all located off one long corridor, with the men's and women's rooms separated by a locked door, to which only Mrs Hughes has the key. These rooms are sparsely furnished compared to the rest of the house – a bed, a chest of drawers, perhaps a wooden chair or two – with few personal decorations. At Downton, the more senior-ranking servants – Carson, Mrs Hughes, Bates and O'Brien – have their own rooms, while everyone else must share. In houses at that time, a servant would often have two beds in their room – either to share with another member of staff or a servant visiting with their employer, so there was less

HIGHCLERE CASTLE

The remarkable Highclere Castle is the location for 'above stairs' at Downton Abbey. The great house sits within a 1,000-acre estate in Berkshire and since 1679 has been home to the Earls of Carnarvon. The turreted castle is, in fact, an envelope built around a Georgian house, which itself contains the medieval monastery that first occupied the site. It stands within parkland designed by Capability Brown between 1774 and 1777 – the execution of which required the relocation of the village. The house was remodelled in 'High Elizabethan' style for the 3rd Earl by Sir Charles Barry (who designed the Houses of Parliament) from 1839 to 1842, with work on the west wing and interiors completed in 1878, after Barry's death.

Mixing architectural styles was not unusual in the nineteenteeth century, so the house combines Italianate effects and Gothic influence. The outside walls are decorated with strapwork designs and cornicing typical of Renaissance architecture, and the great hall, with its arcades and loggias, is modelled on an Italian Renaissance central courtyard, with Gothic curves in the arches. The ground floor has an impressive array of state rooms, including a library filled with over 5650 books, a music room, a smoking room, a south-facing drawing room (in 'rococo revival' style) and a dining room that is dominated by Van Dyck's famous painting of King Charles I. On the first floor are 11 bedrooms – including the Stanhope bedroom, decorated in rich reds for the visit of the Prince of Wales in 1895. The 40 to 50 bedrooms on the other floors are no longer used.

Highclere and Downton share interesting parallels. In 1895, the 5th Earl married an American heiress, Almina Wombwell, rumoured to be the illegitimate daughter of Alfred de Rothschild, who left her his millions. Her money saved the estate and sponsored Howard Carter, who discovered Tutankhamun's tomb in 1922. During the First World War, Highclere was also a military hospital, with Almina herself heading the nursing staff.

sense of a room being their own, although some might dress it up with pictures on the walls or a cheerful rug. But most would have some personal mementoes such as a family photograph or a favourite book.

In the basement, the warren of rooms would be functional in form and character. Painted in almost military hues of pale greens, greys and browns, each room would be designated a specific use. When the houses were large and the servants were plentiful, this could reach almost ridiculous proportions – perhaps the most extreme was Kinmel Hall at Clwyd in Wales, built 1871–6 with 52 main bedrooms, quarters for 60 live-in staff and a room used only for ironing newspapers.

VIOLET, THE DOWAGER COUNTESS
'Are we going to have tea, or not?'

The kitchen is at the heart of the operations; with just a few small windows set high up, its heat and noise permeate the walls and corridors that snake around it. The vast coal range with its six or seven ovens on the go ensure that everyone in there is hot and bothered. In the early twentieth century, coal was cheap – around £1 a ton – so burning a hundredweight of coal a day was quite the norm, and there were almost no regulations regarding pollution either. In 1920, it was estimated that 3 per cent of the heat generated by coal was used to warm food and 7 per cent heated hot water. Of the rest, 35 per cent was absorbed by the brickwork, 25 per cent was lost in flue gases and at least 30 per cent went into heating the kitchen – all year round.

Close to the kitchen is a stillroom (for making cakes and jams and for preparing breakfast trays), a scullery (for washing up), a washroom, a flower room, wine and beer cellars, the housemaid's closet (for storing brushes and pails) and even a brushing room (principally for the brushing of muddy hunting clothes). The butler's pantry has a desk and chair for Carson to do his administrative work, or decant the port, but most importantly it has access to the silver safe (which could be a room of its own with a strong door). Mrs Hughes's sitting room is rather more comfortable, with a fireplace and an armchair or two, but it also has a desk so that she can draw up her complicated rotas for the staff and for the linens, as well as keep up the accounts for the kitchen stores.

Wartime menus

The footman Gordon Grimmett remembered the sophistication of food at Longleat during the First World War: 'We fed very well at Longleat; indeed as visiting servants reminded us, "You wouldn't know there was a war on." Each week three sheep of different breeds were butchered for the household, a Southdown, Westmoreland and a Brittany. We also had pheasant, partridge, goose, venison, hare and rabbit. Rarely was beef served. The meat course was followed by a variety of puddings and cheese. Since there was no gas or electricity all food was cooked on charcoal. Again, Longleat was the only place I served in where there was a fish still. In it swimming about were pike or trout in their season. They were caught in lakes on the estate and put in the still to cleanse them of the taste of mud.'

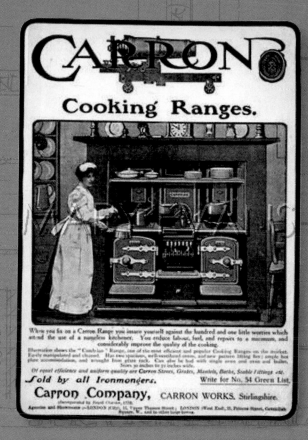

Surviving shooting parties

Daisy, Countess of Warwick (right), was a society beauty and mistress of King Edward VII who found no joy in shooting parties: 'My husband was such a crack shot that we were asked everywhere ... The average party might number sixteen, as too many guns spoil the shoot. We began the day by breakfasting at ten o'clock ...The men went out shooting and then came the emptiness of the long morning from which I suffered silently. I can remember the groups of women sitting discussing their neighbours or writing letters at impossible little ornamental tables ...There were a few unsporting men asked – "darlings". These men of witty and amusing conversation were always asked as extras everywhere to help entertain the women; otherwise we should have been left high and dry. The "ladies" ... rarely took part in the shoot, not even going out to join the shooters until luncheon time. Then, dressed in tweeds and trying to look as sportsmanlike as the clothes of the day allowed, we went out together to some rendezvous of the shooters.'

For the staff at Downton Abbey, the servants' hall is the centre of their lives. It is their dining room but also a kind of communal sitting-room – if a servant had a few minutes to themselves, they would sit there, perhaps do some mending or polishing, and use the opportunity to gossip with the others, until such a moment as the bell rang, summoning them back to work. Any visitors of equal rank to the lower servants would also sit there, but those with the ranking of senior servants would be given the housekeeper's room or butler's pantry. The kitchen courtyard could also provide a little privacy and respite from the constant bustle of work inside; Thomas and O'Brien can frequently be found out there, having a cigarette or two and plotting their latest scheme.

While the house in all its architectural splendour demonstrated the family's wealth and nobility, the land was the reason they loved living there. The aristocracy was a sporting race; a strict calendar for hunting, shooting and fishing provided the very structure for their lives.

As with many other things at that time, it was King Edward VII who set the example. When a prince, he bought the country estate Sandringham in 1862, partly to get away from the stifling influence of his mother. There he held big shooting parties: in November 1905, the nine or ten guns (a man in a shooting party is called a 'gun') brought down a total of 6448 birds in three days, from pheasants to pigeons, plus 232 hares and 576 rabbits. But while shooting parties were considered great sporting fun for the men, for the women they could be deadly dull, with little to do in the day except join the guns for lunch.

A shooting lunch in the early twentieth century might have been simply a sandwich or it could mean an elaborate picnic with hampers and wine coolers carried out by the servants. Shoots meant extra work for the servants; not just the preparing of *al fresco* lunches but also the enormous breakfasts, the brushing of the sporting outfits, the cleaning of the muddy boots and the hanging, plucking and gutting of the birds.

Of course, the sporting calendar also provided employment. Country house owners would employ gamekeepers to protect their birds from poachers: by 1911 there were twice as many gamekeepers in rural areas as there were policemen. A head keeper could also enjoy a generous boost to his income from tips from the guns.

The first day of November opened the hunting season. Unlike shooting, this was a sport for both men and women. It was perhaps one of the only fields in which a woman could directly compete with a man and not be considered 'unfeminine'; she might even be rather admired. Indeed, the women were arguably the more skilled as they had to ride side-saddle (this began to gradually fall out of fashion after the First World War). Furthermore, she could ride out without being chaperoned – something which enabled Mary to flirt dangerously with Kemal Pamuk.

War put a temporary stop to shooting as a sport, and on their return for some men it was no longer the same. Daisy Warwick wrote: 'Men friends – themselves crack shots – have told me that although they formerly enjoyed the shooting season, they no longer can find pleasure in killing birds or ground game, from a new feeling of reluctance to take life of any kind.'

EDITH

'Oh, you know Mary.
She likes to be in at the kill.'

While the sporting activities were for the pleasure of the family and its guests only, the grounds could also provide the setting for fêtes and fairs, which were for everybody, of all classes, to enjoy. 'These houses were built to be the power hub of the neighbourhood,' says Julian. 'They were built to hold local court. So the village fairs and garden parties are a descendant of an older form of party than the house party. When the great milord arrived at his palace, word would go out – "the marquess is at home" – and all the neighbouring gentry would come and more or less pay homage and there would be great feasting for all the locals. In short, it was a demonstration of local power, it wasn't in order to have some nice couple over you'd met at a dinner party. It was to show Shropshire, or wherever, who was running it.'

This kind of celebration went on into the early twentieth century. In 1913, Lord and Lady Armstrong at Cragside held festivities lasting several days to celebrate the twenty-first birthday of their son and heir, The Hon. William Watson-Armstrong – including a ball for staff and townspeople and a garden party the following day, before the family moved to their other seat at Bambrugh Castle for yet more celebrations. Bunting floated from every house in the town, church bells were rung and commemorative mugs were given to schoolchildren. In many ways, the event

Michelle Dockery is Mary

'There's an independence about Mary – she's not influenced by anyone and she's very much her own person, she makes her own decisions. I understand her because I'm one of three girls too and I've always been defiant that I didn't want to do what they did.'

Behind the scenes

For the scenes in the first series, when staff and family went to the fair, the art department hired the Old Tyme Fun Fair, which set up old-fashioned side stalls and a vintage Helter Skelter (built around 1900) as well as playing traditional background organ music to add an authentic atmosphere.

was marked rather like a special and significant occasion for the Royal family is now.

At other times of the year the family would hold a fête or garden party in its grounds to raise money for charity – usually the local hospital fund or the war effort – or simply to celebrate the arrival of the summer. A fair in the village saw the family, servants and locals alike all coming together in the same marquee. With little in the way of a social life for the servants, the fair was big news – a chance to get out of their uniforms, drink a glass of beer or home-made lemonade and flirt and joke with their colleagues. There were coconut shies, tombolas and merry-go-rounds. Sweet stalls were laden with peppermint creams, ices, toffee, fudge, barley sugar, aniseed balls and honeycombs.

In her book *Etiquette of Good Society*, Lady Colin Campbell devoted a whole chapter on how to hold a good garden party. 'See that the gardens and grounds are in perfect order – not a leaf to be seen on the neatly-cut, freshly-rolled lawns and walks; not a single weed in the trim flower beds. Tents of various picturesque forms can be erected here and there for refreshments; a small band of musicians with stringed instruments, or a company of glee-singers hidden from general view, can discourse sweet music at intervals and enliven the scene … The day is concluded by a moonlight dance on the lawn, or in one of the tents, and the garden and grounds are sometimes illuminated with Chinese lanterns and small coloured lamps hung in festoons from the trees, which make the evening scene as picturesque as that of the morning.'

But even a great house like Downton Abbey is not immune to the effects of a new emerging society, and the changes that were occurring in the outside world soon begin to infiltrate its walls, most significantly during the First World War. As war begins, the family decide that they must contribute directly to the war effort and convert a large part of the house to accommodate convalescing officers. Practically speaking, this restructuring of the great house is simple enough to achieve, but the harder change to bear is the different role that the family now has within their own home. Robert no longer feels he is the master of his own domain and there is confusion for everybody as to who is really in charge. Only Sybil, changing from her nurse's uniform into evening dress for supper with the family, has clear lines to cross. But she must learn to live a new life as someone who attends the needs of others alongside her role as the daughter of an earl.

The changing face of the aristocracy

By the end of 1914 alone, the First World War had done away with six peers, 16 baronets, six knights, 95 sons of peers, 82 sons of baronets and 84 sons of knights. Higher taxes and falling incomes meant that many families were forced to sell their ancestral homes. Death duties, which increased to up to 40 per cent in 1919 and continued to rise, also sounded the final knell for some. A fifth of the land in Scotland, some four million acres, came on the market after the First World War.

At Downton, the library becomes the recreation room for the officers, with card tables set out and comfortable chairs. The drawing room is a dormitory: white metal bedsteads line the walls, incongruous below the oil paintings. The great hall is filled with tables for the officers and nurses as a sort of administration centre. The family, used to spreading itself out languorously over the ground floor, must now restrict itself to the dining room, small library and boudoir.

LORD GRANTHAM

'You see a million bricks that may crumble, a thousand gutters and pipes that may block and leak, and stone that will crack in the frost … I see my life's work.'

Even when the war is finally over, it is not going to be as simple as moving the furniture to get the house back to normal. For many families their homes were irrevocably changed – and not just because so many of the young heirs had been killed. Downton Abbey has the money to survive, thanks to Cora, and it hopes the question of its inheritance is settled with Matthew. But Robert knows better than to feel at ease when it comes to the preservation of his family's house. He may not have a job in the ordinary sense of the word, but his life's work will never be over; even his death will not signal the end. It will simply mean he has moved aside for his successor to continue.

My dear Matt...
of you constant...
terrible hardsh...
be facing. How b...
what good fortu...
you command...
...officer

Romance

CHAPTER SEVEN

Matthew: 'Shall I remind you of some of the choicest remarks you made about me when I arrived here? Because they live in my memory as fresh as the day they were spoken.'

Mary: 'Oh, Matthew. What am I always telling you? You must pay no attention to the things I say.'

When they kiss, it is a long kiss, all the more passionate for being delayed far longer than it should have been.

*W*hen Mary and Matthew Crawley finally kiss, it seems that their complex relationship has at last found a resolution. In that moment they certainly intend to be together – Matthew proposes and Mary accepts.

However, the complications of their situation, from the expectations of their families to the issue of class, the advent of war and their own fiery natures, mean the conclusion of their story is, as yet, far from being reached.

Mary, as the daughter of an earl, has long expected to marry a man of equal, if not senior, rank to her father. She has always known that she would never inherit the title or the estate at Downton in her own right. If she had married Patrick, the son of her father's heir (his cousin James Crawley), she could have stayed at Downton as his wife, and it would have been her child who would have been next in line for the inheritance. The tragic deaths of father and son on board the *Titanic* put paid to that idea, but it had never been a certainty that Mary would marry him anyway. Mary wants a marriage that brings her a career; one that gives her a life that is possibly even better than the one to which she is accustomed. Marrying a man with a title and estate of even greater significance than Downton Abbey would make relinquishing her claim to it very much easier. A subsequent suitor, the Duke of Crowborough, with all the material wealth and possessions he had to offer, would have suited her very well indeed. (Although, as we know, she had a lucky escape when he scarpered after he realised she would not be inheriting the family fortune.)

Matthew's beliefs are at first difficult for Mary to stomach, but as long as he is her father's heir, he is a desirable suitor, to Mary's parents and

MARY

'I don't have to think about it. Marry a man
who can barely hold his knife like a gentleman?'

Michelle Dockery is Mary

'Mary feels she should have been a boy and then everything would have been so much easier. She fights against her femininity in a way.'

later to Mary, herself. It is only when he risks surrendering his position to Cora's unborn baby, that she sees him once more as he was when he first arrived at Downton, an upper middle class lawyer, with no fortune and a life of commuting ahead of him. She hesitates and, in hesitating, loses him.

Yet Mary should not be written off as callous. She wants, *expects*, to walk down the aisle to a man she loves, but, in the manner of most girls of her class, she tries only to meet the kind of man with whom she and her family deem it suitable for her to fall in love.

VIOLET, THE DOWAGER COUNTESS
'We need to get her settled before the bloom is quite gone off the rose.'

Julian Fellowes explains: 'By the end of the nineteenth century it had been recognised that on the whole marriages were more successful if the couple got on. The arranged marriage, which was still going on to a degree in the eighteenth century, had rather died out. What the English preferred to do was to say, "This is the catchment – now it's up to you to select one of them." That was the principle of the Season.'

Of course, it was not simply Mary's desires that counted when it came to finding her a husband. Getting her settled as soon as possible once she had turned 18 was the driving force of Cora's life – much as it had been for Mrs Bennet in Jane Austen's *Pride and Prejudice* – for she knew that even for an aristocratic woman like her daughter, with every possible privilege, the way to freedom came through marriage. It was the only arrangement that would provide a power base from which she could take charge of her own life, otherwise she would remain trapped behind the heavy front door of Downton Abbey – her home, even though she could not claim a single brick of it.

The concept of marriage bringing freedom may seem strange to us in the twenty-first century, but it was as much about providing a woman with an identity, one that she was unable to claim as long as she lived with her parents. Having been a pawn in her mother's match-making games and required to dress and act demurely in her father's house and unable to travel anywhere without a chaperone, a woman was more or less able to write her own rules once married. Of course, for some this was easier than for others. The young heiress Consuelo Vanderbilt was told by her husband, the Duke of Marlborough, that she was nothing more than 'a link in the chain', which pretty clearly illustrates the shackles that bound her. But for the most part a married woman could host her own parties and choose her guests. In London especially this was no small thing; society hostesses shaped politics and a man who wanted to do well in the capital needed a wife who could confidently manage the circle of people who would push him up the ladder.

MARY

'How many times am I to be ordered to marry the man sitting next to me at dinner?'

CORA

'As many times as it takes.'

The prospects of Cora's younger daughters, Edith and Sybil, would also have been of concern to their mother, but it took serious ambition to marry them all off well. Not that it couldn't be done; the Dowager Duchess of Abercorn was said to have ordered all six of her daughters to marry into the peerage – and no one beneath an earl. Indeed, all three daughters of the 'Double Duchess' (so-called because she married the Duke of Manchester, then had a long affair with the Duke of Devonshire, whom she married after her first husband had died) married very high-ranking peers. When one of these daughters was asked how their mother had achieved such advantageous marriages, she replied: 'We were told that it was only *real* love with an elder son.'

To begin with, the field from which Mary could choose her potential husband was narrow. Dukes, as the highest-ranking hereditary peers in society, were the most sought after, but less than 30 exist and the likelihood of more than one or two of them having an elder son ready for marriage at just the right time was pretty small. So once the Duke of Crowborough was off the scene, Mary needed to look further afield. Cora and Violet would have to ponder which eligible bachelors fitted the bill amongst the few thousand families they knew who constituted

Love and the marriage game

When the enormously rich heiress the Hon. Daisy Maynard (shown here) was 17 years old, in 1879, it was decided that she would marry Prince Leopold – a plan sanctioned by Queen Victoria. However, Daisy was in love with Lord Brooke, as he was with her. The Prince understood, as he was himself in love with someone else. 'We then made plans about telling the Queen,' wrote Daisy, Countess of Warwick. 'It was arranged that the Prince was to break the news to her about my love for Lord Brooke. Her Majesty agreed that first love was sacred, "the divinest thing in the world", indeed, the only true happiness. She would have liked another arrangement, but as my affections were engaged, she would not think of trying to influence me.'

My Dear Mary,

It was such a
you in London. So
you see the wonder
of everything and
our conversation abou
and all its attractu

It is never cl
opportunities might
I do hope occasion
a reason for us to
On such an occasion
so much to ask yo
perhaps we can p
future adventures.

Yours since

Evely

the power stronghold of England. The Season offered the best opportunity to meet the right man, but once that was over country sports provided a good cover to host parties which would impress potential beaux. The family matriarchs would use the excuse of hunting and shooting to invite any eligible sons to stay and meet the daughters of the house. The men could accept such an invitation without embarrassment, and if nothing came of the event, everyone could pretend that the Saturday-to-Monday party had been about sporting intentions only.

Once the intended gentleman was in sight, courtship was a strangely public affair. No woman could spend time with a man unchaperoned, so conversations in which they would try to glean whether or not they had things in common, let alone fall in love, could be conducted only with someone else listening in. Julian once remarked to his great-aunt that it was absurd a woman couldn't be left alone with a man – as if they were *all* going to make a pass. 'Yes, dear,' she said, 'but you were furious if they didn't!' In this world of propriety, letters were the only way in which courting couples could talk intimately. How relieved Mary was to get her encouraging letter from Evelyn Napier – the written word could indicate serious intent in a way that was hard to convey in public small talk.

EDITH

'So he slipped the hook.'

MARY

'At least I'm not fishing with no bait.'

As for Matthew – what are his expectations of love and marriage? When he was a solicitor from Manchester he would not have brooked any parental interference; he wished to marry a girl of his choice and he would have expected to marry for love. However, once he had been named as the heir to the earldom, the pressure was on for him to marry Mary: an idea to which he felt both resistance and temptation in almost equal measure. In a way, the marriage game was now made easier for Matthew; a man was expected to bring the material wealth to a marriage, and with Downton Abbey in his future, he could certainly promise that to any bride. Still, as a romantic and a liberal, he would not want the question of his inheritance to influence the decision of the woman he loved as

Laura Carmichael is Edith

'Edith suffers the heartbreak of not being the favourite daughter and not getting the opportunities that the others have. After losing out on Strallan [right], I think she feels that was it – that was her chance. In a way, during the war she has a kind of freedom from all that and can instead give herself to a noble cause.'

to whether or not she would marry him. Matthew wants a union of mind and soul, not a contract; so when Matthew suspects a mercenary aspect to Mary's decision, he withdraws his proposal. Of course, the reason Mary cannot give Matthew the answer he would like is because her shameful secret is burning a hole in her conscience. Accepting Kemal Pamuk – a man whom she had met only that day – into her room for the night was in itself a shocking act, but for him then to die in her bed… At that moment, Mary's fear would not have been so much for his death as for the entire household and the world beyond it knowing what she had done.

Cast adrift, Mary needs to change tack. She knows that if her scandalous secret got out it would reduce her marriageable options to almost nothing; she has to act quickly and decisively. Sir Richard Carlisle comes into her life and Mary realises the possibilities he brings with him. As for Sir Richard, he sees that he can give her the powerbase she wants and that in turn she would be a brilliant team mate for his ambitious plans. The match of his money and power with her class and beauty would make them a formidable couple in the changing world.

Yet, the Edwardian period was not puritanical in its attitude towards relations between married men and women. Amongst the upper classes in particular, unmarried women did not have sex, but amongst certain sets married women often became mistresses to rich and powerful men once they had had their children. The more sexually liberal behaviour of the time was perhaps a backlash against the harsh morality of Queen Victoria's reign. Her son, King Edward VII, certainly had a number of affairs, a situation well known by his subjects and even sympathised with to a degree. There's the story of a time when Mrs Keppel, the King's much admired and married mistress, was urgently summoned to the country. Stepping into the hansom cab with her luggage, she gave the name of the station: 'King's Cross.' 'Is he? Oh dear,' said the cabby, whipping up his horse.

Even so, the attitude towards relationships between men and women was far from being a case of 'anything goes'. The magnitude of what has happened – in Mary's view – cannot be underestimated. Anita Leslie, herself the daughter of a noble Irish family, spelled out the rules of play in her book *Edwardians In Love*: 'Girls must remain virginal and ignorant. Once married, a young woman could be eyed thoughtfully, but it would not be *de rigueur* to attempt to waylay her before she produced a few sons to carry on her husband's name and inherit his estates.'

Michelle Dockery is Mary

'Mary's really hard in the beginning and she has a tough exterior like her grandmother, but underneath she's vulnerable and I discovered that as we went along. She starts off two-dimensional but after the incident with Kemal, carrying this dark secret, she's a whole person. She was complacent up to that point and now she cares more about other people.'

Despite the louche tales of some of the aristocracy and the Bohemian sets, this was still an age in which it was considered risqué for a woman merely to walk across Hyde Park without a maid to chaperone her. Winston Churchill's cousin, Clare Frewen, did and was told that no nice man would want to marry her after that. Sex as a single woman was considered the ultimate debauchery, a fact of which Mary was left in no doubt. 'If it gets around and you're not already married, every door in London will be slammed in your face,' her mother tells her.

ROSAMUND

'I'm sorry you haven't received more invitations. But then, after four Seasons, one is less a debutante than a survivor.'

Knowing what Mary would really have understood of sex is hard to gauge, however. Women then could hardly write down their ideas on sex before they were married for fear of anyone discovering the text (or, if they did, such diaries were almost invariably destroyed later). Among young women like the Crawley sisters, any practical experience would be very rare, but they would not have been entirely innocent of carnal secrets. Lady Diana Manners writes that she was always a good girl, God-fearing and never telling a lie, until 'with the advent of the young men – benign serpents – came the apple. Though it was never offered or nibbled, I felt guilt at my pleasurable excitement, and a practice of deceit began – hidden letters, denial of hand-holding (my mother felt strongly on this score), and many little lies to save her disappointment in me.'

What a young girl knew of marriage would have been dependent on what their older, more experienced relatives could bring themselves to relate. As one might imagine, this could be quite a shy-making event. Daisy, Countess of Warwick, asserted that: 'Society girls, if not as innocent as they were "pure", were often unbelievably ignorant even of the physical facts of marriage. Marriage – their goal, their destiny, their desire – was all in a rosy haze.' My own grandmother, Olwen, was called into her mother's sitting-room a few days before her wedding. She was asked if she knew that 'Peregrine would have new and different expectations of the relationship after the marriage,' and Olwen replied that yes, she did know. Her mother then said: 'My generation cannot speak on this subject with any ease, but there is one important thing you should know,' which made her daughter pause with nervous apprehension before she heard: 'It's terrific fun!' This certainly would have taken the fear out of it for a virgin bride, which is rather sweet. The details of the act were perhaps often best left out. An aunt of my step-grandmother's was taken into the garden to have marriage explained to her: 'How perfectly disgusting!' she exclaimed, before storming back into the house and cancelling her wedding. She died a spinster. Julian likes the story of the daughter of a Yorkshire earl who sent a postcard to her sister from her honeymoon, saying: 'Marriage is lovely, but, cor, ain't it rude?'

Girlish dreams of love and meeting 'The One' were found then, as now, in contemporary novels. Victorian writers such as the Brontë sisters (*Jane Eyre, Wuthering Heights*) and the poet Christina Rossetti continued to find an appreciative audience in the Edwardians. In their own time, *Howard's End*, by E.M. Forster, which explores the idea of cross-class relationships, was published in 1910 and was his first big hit; and Edith Wharton's *The House of Mirth*, the story of an anti-heroine torn between the need for a rich husband and the dream of marrying for love, sold 140,000 copies when it was published in 1905. The increasing numbers of tabloid newspapers and their lurid tales of princes and showgirls doubtless also fuelled many a romantic fantasy.

Inspiring the rather more erotic desires of young girls was the hugely popular novelist Elinor Glyn. She was introduced to society by her friend Daisy Warwick, herself a lover of King Edward VII. Glyn wrote racy novels that scandalized Edwardians. Her 1907 bestseller *Three Weeks* was supposedly based on her affair with Lord Alastair Innes-Ker, brother of the Duke of Roxburghe, and inspired the doggerel:

Would you sin
With Elinor Glyn
On a tiger skin?
Or would you prefer
To err with her
On some other fur?

For all the changes rippling in the undercurrent, marriage was still a necessity for the female sex of the upper classes, so Cora finds it hard to sympathise with Mary when she refuses Matthew because she herself had

The Marlborough House Set

Daisy, Countess of Warwick, was one of the leading members of the Marlborough House Set – intimates of the King who were well-known for their spouse-swapping activities: 'There was plenty of tolerance for both sexes, but it was not so diagnosed perhaps. In my circle there was a kind of freemasonry of conduct. We could be and do as we liked according to the code. The unforgiveable sin was to give away any member of our group. That was class loyalty, I suppose, but we had no name for it.'

Wills's Cigarettes

Elinor Glyn

Servants seeking love

Margaret Powell was a housemaid in the 1920s, but her life below stairs was not so different from Daisy's just a few years earlier. 'The business of getting a young man was not respectable and one's employers tended to degrade every relationship. It seemed to me one was expected to find husbands under a gooseberry bush. Their daughters were debs and they could meet young men at balls, dances and private parties, but if any of the servants had boyfriends they were known as "followers"... You had to slink up the area steps and meet on the corner of the road on some pretext like going to post a letter.'

not had a love match. She accepted Robert because her mother wished her to marry an English nobleman, and he chose her because he needed her money to save Downton Abbey. Cora might have wished for love in her marriage – and she was fortunate in that it wasn't long before she had it – but it wouldn't have been her priority, and in that she was not unusual. Most of the American Buccaneers were doing the same thing.

However, not everyone was prepared to go through the rigmarole of a formal courtship when they knew their ultimate goal. In 1901 an advertisement in the *Daily Telegraph* read: 'An English Peer of very old title is desirous of marrying at once a very wealthy lady, her age and looks are immaterial, character must be irreproachable; she must be a widow or a spinster – not a divorcee. If among your clients you know such a lady, who is willing to purchase the rank of a peeress for £25,000 sterling, paid in cash to her future husband, and who has sufficient wealth besides to keep up the rank of a peeress, I shall be pleased if you will communicate with me in the first instance by letter when a meeting can be arranged in your office.'

DAISY

'Thomas is lovely, in't he? He's funny and handsome. He's got such lovely teeth.'

While the family at Downton are involved in marital machinations, love is blossoming below stairs. Curiously, despite the fact that they lived and worked in close quarters, romance between the servants of a house was not a very frequent thing. Perhaps they were too busy, but more likely the butler and the housekeeper, who saw themselves as the protectors of their staff's moral behaviour, strictly forbade such goings on. If two servants did marry, they would almost certainly have to leave service. It was only in exceptional circumstances, where the family did not want either of them to leave, that arrangements would be made to keep them on – perhaps a cottage in the grounds for them to live in, or permission would be given for the husband to stay, with his wife living elsewhere.

It was almost impossible to find a suitor or beau outside the workplace if you were a servant, simply because there were so few opportunities to do so. Time off could be a rare thing if you had a position such as valet or lady's maid, as you would be at the beck and call of your master or mistress and would have to travel with them wherever they went. If you were a maid or footman you were entitled to very little free time, and holidays were almost non-existent if you were cook, housekeeper or butler. Even on a day off, strict rules meant that female staff had to be back at the house by ten o'clock at night. Gentlemen callers would only very occasionally have been allowed to come for them at the house's back door: 'No followers allowed' was the usual cry. Unless marriage was a definite prospect, a suitor could forget a warm welcome from his sweetheart's boss. But for the women, just as for their counterparts upstairs, marriage represented freedom and was therefore a highly sought prize.

ANNA

'Because I love you, Mr Bates. I know it's not ladylike to say it, but I'm not a lady and I don't pretend to be.'

For all the rules, no one can entirely prevent a kitchenmaid developing a crush on a handsome, liveried footman, or the mutual admiration that grows between a capable housemaid and a kindly valet. And with almost no social life to speak of, the servants had to take their chances – not to mention stolen kisses – where they could. Rosina Harrison, who had a long career as a lady's maid, wrote in her memoir *My Life In Service* of visits to other houses with her first mistress:

'At first I found these servants' halls rather frightening. There was an awful silence during a meal but I soon found out that some sort of conversation would be taking place between the sexes by the playing of footsy-footsy under the table. The blushes and the occasional giggles gave this away.'

Daisy doesn't have the time to think much beyond the next task she's been set by Mrs Patmore, but when she looks up and sees the handsome face of Thomas, the footman, her own romantic daydreams are sparked. How did a girl like Daisy learn of these romantic ideals? There was no cinema yet – they were in the big cities but not in rural outposts – and she would rarely have an hour or two to herself to read even a 'penny dreadful' (the lurid story serials). But she would know songs. Music was a hugely popular form of entertainment – from the music halls of the working

Joanne Froggatt is Anna

'She probably just plugs along and plays the cards she's been given. I don't think she's a romantic dreamer. She's pragmatic – quite matter-of-fact about things.'

ILLEGITIMACY

Margaret Powell, a housemaid in the 1920s, was determined to marry (spinsters were derided as 'lacking practically everything') but soon learnt that, in her position, this wasn't going to be easy. When Powell's colleague, an under-parlourmaid called Agnes, got pregnant by the mistress's nephew, all the maids were subjected to a long lecture by their employer on the 'evils of such wanton behaviour', and told that no nice young man would suggest such a thing to a girl he hoped to marry. 'Well now, that's another ridiculous remark,' she wrote, 'because the ratio of girls to young men was so high that if you had a young man and you cared about him and he suggested this, it seemed to be the only way to keep him. You had a hard job not to do it if you were not going to be stuck without a young man at all, and if you were dying to get out of domestic service, which most of us were.' When eventually she did marry, she had another disappointment in store: 'The employers always claimed that the training they gave you stood you in good stead when you left and married and had a family of your own. When I left domestic service I took with me the knowledge of how to cook an elaborate seven-course dinner and an enormous inferiority complex; I can't say that I found those an asset to my married life.'

classes to the string quartets that played at aristocratic dinner parties. A major event would be quickly retold in song form (after the sinking of the *Titanic*, piano sheet music could be bought that would 'tell' the story of the tragedy). There were popular dances and steps to learn, too, which provided the perfect excuse for a man to grab his sweetheart and hold her tightly around the waist, as William would have done with Daisy, if Thomas hadn't got in first when they were dancing 'The Grizzly Bear'.

Rosina Harrison writes: 'Marriage was the goal of nearly every woman servant. It wasn't easy for them. After the war, men were scarce, the demand far outweighed the supply and a maid's limited and irregular time off was an added disadvantage. Then there was the having to be back by ten o'clock which made every date like Cinderella's ball, only you didn't lose your slipper, you could lose your job. There was no status in being in service, you were a nobody; marriage was the way out of it. Strangely, there was not a lot of intermarriage between servants.'

When Anna meets Bates she is Head Housemaid and well on her way to a successful career – if she stayed on at Downton Abbey she could expect to take over from Mrs Hughes. Had she given up on love? A woman who wanted a career couldn't have marriage too, but Anna and Bates slowly develop a relationship based on friendship and mutual respect, and when she falls in love with him, says Julian, 'she decides she's going to marry him come hell or high water.' Bates seems to be just as in love with her, but his past makes him opaque about his feelings for a long time. Of course, the other obstacle is that he is still married and must try to apply for a divorce.

Divorce was a thorny issue, not least because the legal machinery required to achieve it was slow and complicated. A man could divorce a woman only if he could prove her adultery, while a woman had to prove her husband had committed bigamy, incest or adultery with cruelty or unreasonable desertion of more than two years. But more off-putting than the legal complications of divorce was the social stigma attached to it, particularly for women. In 1912, just 587 couples in England and Wales were divorced; by 1919 that number had risen to 1654, but this was still a tiny percentage of the general population.

Many women of the middle and upper classes resisted divorce because without their husbands they would have almost no social life. A divorced woman could find herself shunned by Society, and when she was no longer invited to smart dinners, let alone dances, her opportunities for friendship dwindled. In a further dash to her fortunes, unless she had a man

HOMOSEXUALITY

Thomas, the footman, treads a dangerous path when he attempts to revive an affair with the Duke of Crowborough; the duke's nastiness threatens to be the least of his troubles. His sexuality seems to be known by some of the staff, as Mrs Patmore tries to explain to a hopelessly infatuated Daisy: 'He's not a ladies' man'. But that is not to say that the threat of a prison sentence did not loom large: he would always have to be careful in his relationships.

Thomas is, as Julian Fellowes explains, 'one of those people who feels he has been born into a position that is far beneath his capabilities. He is clever and good-looking. But every so often he gets caught out – as he is by the Duke. Perhaps he is not as clever as he thinks he is . He is gay. It doesn't trouble him – he just knows that to get on in this world he has to be circumspect. But he mustn't be thought of as hating it as Bates hates his limp. He just wants to be happy without having to be put in prison for it.'

DUKE OF CROWBOROUGH

'And who'll believe a greedy footman over the words of a duke? If you're not careful, you'll end up behind bars.'

Although there had been a law against sodomy since 1533, homosexual acts between men were only explicitly and severely legislated against in 1885; it was for this law that Oscar Wilde was indicted in 1896. The hysteria surrounding the Wilde case greatly affected the general view of homosexuality, but there were some notable cases where it was ignored if not benignly accepted. Edward Carpenter was a member of the Edwardian intelligentsia, a writer who openly admitted to being gay (or 'Uranian' as he coined it) and lived with a working-class man from Sheffield for many years. Carpenter's books were investigated by the police for suspect moral content, but he was never sent to prison. There did exist a subculture of gay life but this was not in any way tolerated by mainstream society, and homosexual acts – or the suspicion of them – frequently did lead to imprisonment.

12 TONS

MARY

'Richard Carlisle is powerful. He's rich and getting richer. He wants to buy a proper house, you know, with an estate. He says after the war the market will be flooded and we can take our pick.'

already waiting for her, a divorced woman would be most unlikely to ever marry again.

In the upper classes adultery was so common in certain sets as to hardly raise an eyebrow. There was a popular maxim: 'Never comment on a likeness', meaning you should not remark upon the likeness of a baby to a man you knew in case he was indeed its father! An adulterous divorcee had even more to lose if she had children, for custody would be granted to the father. Lady Colin Campbell enjoyed married life and high status in the 1880s, but after her husband took her to court for adultery with four co-respondents she lost almost all her friends. Thanks to her beauty and wit she found a new, happier, life amongst literary and artistic sets.

The working classes bore 'huge numbers' of children out of wedlock (we know this thanks to social data collected in the early twentieth century), while the middle classes were, on the whole, much more reactionary, refusing any notion of illegitimacy.

In even countenancing the notion of marrying the divorced Bates, Anna shows considerable mettle. But she's in love. 'I can't think of anything but him. It's as if I were mad, or ill … I suppose that's what love is,' she says. 'A kind of illness. And when you've got it, there's just nothing else.' Whether above or below stairs, the illness catches them just the same.

'IF YOU WERE THE ONLY GIRL IN THE WORLD', WRITTEN IN 1916.

Sometimes when I feel low and things look blue
I wish a boy I had … say one like you.
Someone within my heart to build a throne
Someone who'd never part, to call my own

If you were the only girl in the world and I were the only boy
Nothing else would matter in the world today
We could go on loving in the same old way

A garden of Eden just made for two
With nothing to mar our joy
I would say such wonderful things to you
There would be such wonderful things to do
If you were the only girl in the world and I were the only boy.

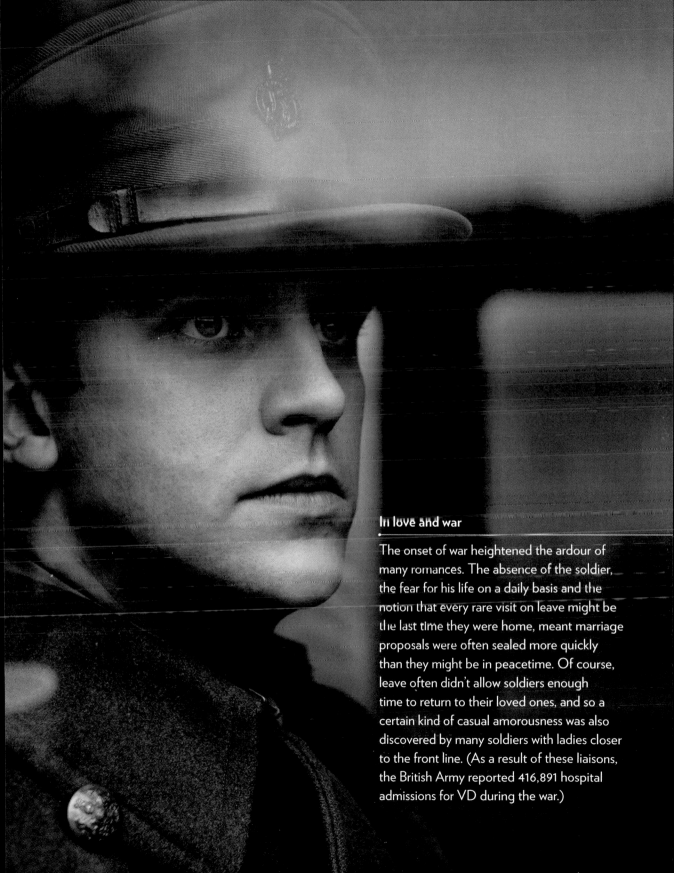

In love and war

The onset of war heightened the ardour of
many romances. The absence of the soldier,
the fear for his life on a daily basis and the
notion that every rare visit on leave might be
the last time they were home, meant marriage
proposals were often sealed more quickly
than they might be in peacetime. Of course,
leave often didn't allow soldiers enough
time to return to their loved ones, and so a
certain kind of casual amorousness was also
discovered by many soldiers with ladies closer
to the front line. (As a result of these liaisons,
the British Army reported 416,891 hospital
admissions for VD during the war.)

War

CHAPTER EIGHT

The air is full of flashes and the noise of guns.
The Somme. November 1916. Men covered from head
to foot in mud are pouring over the side of the trench
and slipping and sliding into its murky,
sodden safety. The last figure, as filthy as
the rest, pulls himself back to his feet.

It is Matthew Crawley.

y 1916, along with hundreds of thousands of others, Matthew Crawley is fighting a war on the front line. The Battle of the Somme, which lasted from July until November of that year, still remains one of the deadliest battles ever seen: almost half a million British soldiers were killed in this offensive – more even than throughout the course of the Second World War.

The days of summer garden parties and formal dinners at Downton Abbey seem a world away, as Matthew grapples with life in the trenches. Here, he is exposed to the harsh reality of the battlefield and yet he is strangely at home as a leader of men. His life has already seen upheaval, having experienced the enormous change in circumstances from being a middle-class lawyer to becoming an earl-in-waiting, but now he is facing another seemingly insurmountable challenge, as he fights to survive as an officer in the trenches.

The advent of the war itself was not a shock. The shifting balance of power within Europe had long heralded a clash of opposing forces, and war loomed on the horizon. The assassination of the heir to the Austro-Hungarian throne, Archduke Franz Ferdinand, in July 1914, triggered the start of the conflict. War was declared by Britain at 11pm on 4 August, as Germany invaded Belgium. The announcement was received with the gravity with which it was made, but no one expected it to last long. Britain entered the fray as an ally of France, who was coming to the aid of the now-occupied neutral country.

The whole of Britain was behind the war effort from the start, believing in the nation's strength as it joined in the European power struggle.

MATTHEW

'At the front, the men pray to be spared, of course. But if that's not to be, they pray for a bullet that kills them cleanly ... For too many of them today, that prayer had not been answered.'

Julian Fellowes on the outbreak of war

'The last scene of the first series, in which Robert announces that war has begun, is taken from an episode in my own father's life. When he was just over two years old there was a great garden party at Hurstborne Park and my father can remember this one moment when a man came out onto the terrace and said, "Ladies and gentlemen, I regret to inform you we are at war with Germany." I said to him afterwards, why do you think you remembered it? It was his first memory, you see. And he said that he could only suppose that the atmosphere changed in such an extraordinary way that even a baby would feel it. So that was it – I just lifted that exact scene for the show.'

POST OFFICE TELEGRAPHS.   No. of Telegram..............

Brass & Stevens-wares, London.

Office Stamp.

If the accuracy of an Inland Telegram be doubted, the telegram will be repeated on payment of half the amount originally paid for its transmission, any fraction of 1d. less than ½d. being reckoned as ½d.; and if it be found that there was any inaccuracy, the amount paid for repetition will be refunded. Special conditions are applicable to the repetition of Foreign Telegrams.

DOWNTON 5 AUG 14.

Charges } to pay   £   s.   d.

Handed } in at   .M.,   Received } here at   .M.

TO { The Earl of Grantham

As of 7pm last night.

Great Britain is at War

with Germany.

Devonshire

TELEGRAM.

R DELIVERY.

rl of Grantham

ton Abbey,

As the cast prepared for the storyline that would dominate series two of Downton Abbey, Alastair Bruce, the programme's historical advisor, explained to the actors that in 1914 the phrase 'For King and Country!' was a very powerful motivator. 'Real enthusiasm caught everyone at the start of the war. They thought it would be quick and they'd have tea and medals for Christmas. They thought there would be glory.'

LORD GRANTHAM

'My Lords, ladies and gentlemen, can I ask for silence? Because I very much regret to announce … that we are at war with Germany.'

Field Marshal Earl Kitchener, Secretary of State for War, was an almost lone voice in believing it would take three years to defeat the German Army. So he planned accordingly, orchestrating the mass recruitment of volunteers with his now iconic 'Your Country Needs You' posters. In 1914 alone, even with the whole of the British Army mobilised, another 1,186,357 men signed up. On the first day of Kitchener's appeal, the press of men around the Central London Recruiting Office was so big that mounted police were deployed to hold them in check. It felt like a huge push in manpower and morale, and many continued to believe that the might of the Allied Armies would be enough to overcome the Austro–Hungarian and German forces quickly.

Lord Kitchener was not alone in encouraging the men to sign up for the war. Admiral Charles Fitzgerald applied pressure to those who had not volunteered their services by founding the Order of the White Feather in 1914; a white feather was a symbol of cowardice, and female members of this group presented these feathers to men who were not in khaki. Such an act was hugely distressing to those men who could not sign up for legitimate reasons, either because of a disability or because they were employed in jobs considered 'essential' for the smooth running of the home front. Vera Brittain witnessed this behaviour at first hand, and wrote that her young uncle was 'killed' by the stress of the war because, although he was desperate to sign up, he was not allowed to leave his work at the bank and, as well as having to do the work of two or three men, therefore suffered the ignominy of not being in uniform. 'I shrink from meeting or speaking to soldiers or soldiers' relatives, and to take an ordinary walk on a Sunday is abominable,' he wrote to her. Men such as Robert, who were older but still physically fit, also felt the pain of being forced to – as they saw it – shirk their moral duty.

Women, too, put pressure on their men to be warriors. Baroness Orczy, a popular romantic novelist at the time, set up an Active Service League in 1915. Twenty thousand women joined the league, pledging not to be seen with any man who had not answered 'his country's call', hoping that by taking this stance they would influence their brothers, friends and sweethearts to sign up. Caught up in the moment, their reasoning may have seemed sound at the time, but what guilt and sadness many of those women must have felt later when they reflected on their campaign.

EDITH

'Of course it is horrid, but when heroes are giving their lives every day, it's hard to watch healthy young men doing nothing.'

Before too long, with increasing casualty numbers and an ever-lengthening forecast for the end of the war, it was apparent that there weren't enough men volunteering in Britain to man the forces, so in 1916 the Military Service Act was passed to introduce conscription. Now there was nothing voluntary about being in the war – it was a legal requirement. All men between the ages of 18 and 41 (this age was later raised) had to register. Conscription put into uniform six million of the ten million men across Britain who were eligible to fight. Unless you were medically unfit, in essential wartime employment, a religious minister or a conscientious objector (which meant you went to prison instead), you had to go to war.

The dream of glory that came with the announcement of war was never fulfilled. Instead, the new advances in technology – powerful artillery, as well as poison gas, aeroplanes and tanks – combined with the war

BRITONS

"WANTS
YOU"

JOIN YOUR COUNTRY'S ARMY!
GOD SAVE THE KING

Reproduced by permission of LONDON OPINION

Conscription

In the build-up to the First World War, the weight of expectation lay heavily upon Britain's young men. Vera Brittain, in her autobiography *The Testament of Youth*, recalled at Uppingham Speech Day in July 1914, when war was on the horizon, 'the final prophetic precept, and the breathless silence which followed the Headmaster's slow, religious emphasis upon the words: "If a man cannot be useful to his country, he is better dead." '

WOMEN OF BRITAIN SAY –
"GO!"

Published by the PARLIAMENTARY RECRUITING COMMITTEE, London.

ISOBEL CRAWLEY

'But this is a war! And we must be in it together!
High and low, rich and poor! There can be no
"special cases" because every man at the front
is a special case to someone!'

being fought on several fronts, meant for a dirtier, deadlier war than even the most experienced military men expected. Out on the front line, trenches were dug to protect the men from machine-gun fire and heavy artillery, but these anticipated places of refuge soon became almost more the enemy than the opposing armies.

For the soldiers on the front line, all life took place within the narrow confines of trenches about seven or eight feet deep, with a sump running along the bottom, covered with duckboards. 'Firesteps' of earth, sandbags or wood enabled a soldier to look out across to enemy lines or even shoot. Very often these steps were a soldier's only place of refuge – a tiny area on which to keep lookout, fight for one's life, grab a bite to eat and try to sleep for a few snatched minutes.

By May 1916 there was an elaborate system of trenches stretching 800km (500 miles) along the Western Front from the English Channel to Switzerland, with just a narrow strip of No Man's Land between them, running many lines deep on either side. Although fighting was hard, the warring countries were deadlocked. The military strategy that became the Battle of the Somme was devised to break this impasse, but the French, who were to lead it, were surprised by a German attack in Verdun, which meant the British were suddenly placed at the forefront of the action instead.

As an officer at the Battle of the Somme, Matthew is caught up in a battlefield situation like no other. On just the first day of fighting the British Army suffered 57,470 casualties, with 19,240 men dead. Most of these casualties occurred in the first hour of the attack.

During his two years at war, Matthew has undergone extraordinary adjustments. Leading his men over the top required nerves of steel and the suppression of a natural fearful instinct. Yet it was not death of which he would be afraid, but the unknown of life as a survivor – whatever happened, come the end of the war and the return to life at home, a man would be changed, physically, mentally or, most likely, both. The cares that dominated Matthew previously – his new-found elevated position in society and broken engagement to Mary – must have faded into insignificance as he led his men into battle. Death was not to be welcomed, but it was almost preferable to life as a wreck of a man. And, of course, in 1916, these men were not to know that they were halfway through the war – it felt then as if it would go on for several more years. That thought alone would have been unendurable.

As well as the death and sickness all around them, the men suffered the extreme hardship of baking heat in the stuffy trenches in summer and freezing cold and damp in winter. Uniforms would be sodden, food was often lukewarm by the time it arrived, and during the hardest battles, when it was most needed, it was delivered only every two days.

The most dreaded duty was sentry watch, which required a man to be awake and alert in the night, and allowed only for a few minutes of sleep at a time. On top of all this, there might be rats 'as big as kittens' running through the trenches, eating the men's bread. In No Man's Land the rats were so large they were said to be able to eat a wounded man unable to defend himself. This may be poetic licence, but they certainly bit the men as they slept. In the trenches in Annequin in 1917, Alexander Stewart was 'much troubled by the rats coming in and licking the brilliantine off my hair; for this reason I had to give up using grease on my head'.

Against all the odds, the soldiers showed immense fortitude and courage. Most poignantly, this is seen in their attempts to recreate some notion of home life in the midst of the unceasing annihilation and squalid conditions. Bulbs and seeds might be planted, birds and rabbits kept as pets. Hollowed-out 'funk holes' in the walls of the trenches, in which a man might lie down with a modicum of comfort and a ground-sheet for privacy, were common. Much better were the dugouts: in 1915 Billie Harris found some British ones on the Somme front 'too killing for words. In one of them there is a lovely case of stuffed birds, a beautiful four-poster bed, and some nice chairs, a good big table, towel horse, ivory wash hand stand etc & endless bric-a-brac.' Most such encampments, of course, were not this luxurious, and while they provided shelter there was always the risk that they would collapse on top of the men if a shell went off nearby.

Parcels sent to the soldiers helped to give them a little taste of home – sometimes quite literally, with packages of home-made plum cake and tinned fruit sent over. Alongside the longed-for letters of news from home, other keenly awaited items included warm clothing, tobacco and chocolate. The Army Postal Service, administered by the Royal Engineers, was extraordinarily efficient in the face of adversity, delivering letters and parcels to the front line daily. The Government had decided that this was an important service which boosted morale for the soldiers. The Home Depot, which sorted all mail bound for the troops, estimated that it handled two billion letters and 114 million parcels during the course of the First World

Conditions at the Somme

In his book *Six Weeks*, John Lewis-Stempel cites Sidney Rogerson's account describing the mud of the Somme, which was bad enough to 'make an ex-public schoolboy drop the habit of understatement'. 'It was like walking through caramel. At every step the foot stuck fast, and was only wrenched out by a determined effort, bringing away with it several pounds of earth till legs ached in every muscle. No one could struggle through that mud for more than a few yards without rest. Terrible in its clinging consistency, it was the arbiter of destiny, the supreme enemy, paralysing and mocking English and German alike. Distances were measured not in yards but in mud.'

Dan Stevens is Matthew

'The war scenes were very exciting to film.
There was a network of trenches and it was
amazingly authentic and incredibly muddy.
It really gave you a sense of the environment
– going over the top, guns firing, bombs
exploding, men shouting and all the while
the cameras are rolling. The adrenaline
really went – it wasn't so much the noise of
the bombs as that you could feel it in your
chest. And then you would look up at the
end of the take to see the crew completely
covered in ash.'

The brotherhood of regiments

The North Riding Volunteers is the name
of Downton Abbey's local regiment. The
army encouraged whole factories, towns and
villages to sign up together because it was
thought that people would fight harder and
feel a greater sense of loyalty and duty if they
were alongside men they knew. Consequently,
when whole regiments from a local area were
sent out during the Somme, all the young
men in a village might be wiped out.

The role of extras

Many of the extras employed for the war
scenes were men who live locally to the
trenches in Ipswich and have worked on
several films set in the war; some even
brought along their own uniforms.

POSTAGE REVENUE
ONE PENNY
My dear Matthew,
We al
of you constantly and
terrible hardships you
be facing. How brave yo
What good fortune fo
you command to hav
an officer.

War. The spoils of a parcel would be shared with close comrades, whether the recipient was dead or alive — although Richard Holmes writes in *Tommy* that one infantry section could not bring itself to eat the twenty-first-birthday cake of a dead comrade and gave it to another, less fastidious, platoon. Letters sent to dead soldiers, however, would be returned.

In spite of – or perhaps because of – all the chaos, the social order of life in the trenches was designed to replicate life back home. Matthew may have felt like a relative commoner in the context of Downton Abbey, but he was in fact an upper middle-class man with a public school education ('probably somewhere like Rugby or Marlborough,' says Julian) and a profession. Because of this background, he would have started his career in the army as an officer, beginning as a Lieutenant and rising to Captain. According to Alastair, 'Social equality would undermine authority on the battlefield and so much of a battle involves unthinking obedience to sustain it'. So the army needed to be confident that the soldiers would follow orders – even when those orders were leading them to almost-certain death. The only way to ensure this was for the men issuing the orders to be a leader that others were happy to follow. Although a concept that is perhaps difficult for us to understand in the twenty-first century, a hundred years ago the idea of everyone knowing their place was not considered derogatory, but simply a fact of life. R. C. Sheriff, author of the seminal play about the First World War *Journey's End*, wrote about the leadership qualities of boys from public schools in his anthology, *Promise of Greatness*.

'In those days, in England, there were class distinctions that everyone recognized and accepted without resentment so long as they were not abused. In civilian life the humble workman was content to obey a foreman who had risen from his own class so long as the boss was socially a cut above the foreman.'

However, soon the problem arose that the supply of the right 'officer material' was dwindling. Officers in the First World War had a greater chance of dying than a private soldier – their average life expectancy on the front line was assumed to be six weeks. To maintain the numbers, men from the lower ranks had to be promoted: at the beginning of the war just two per cent of officers had risen through the ranks; by 1918 this figure was about 40 per cent, the newcomers generally coming from lower middle class backgrounds. Their promotion made them 'temporary gentlemen' and as such they were entitled to the privileges and respect accorded to gentlemen in civilian life. Thomas, the footman at Downton, enjoys a small taste of this fast-track rise through the ranks, both in the army and at home. However, this promotion was to last only for the duration of the war, and when they returned to civilian life, many men found it a shock that they were suddenly stripped of their new-found status.

Of course, in the line of fire such differences of rank could be forgotten. Men facing death together became bonded in a way that no one else would be able to understand – certainly not anyone back home. Matthew and his fellow officers become especially close to their 'batmen', soldiers who perform valet-like duties. Bates was Robert's batman in the Boer War, which explains much of the empathy the two subsequently share, despite the chasm between them in class status that would never normally permit such a friendship. A batman would free up the officer to concentrate on his military activities by tending to his daily needs – cleaning his kit, cooking his food, carrying his case. In return, the batman would be relieved of the much-hated sentry duties and would earn 15s a month.

Amazingly, despite the boredom, drudgery, increasing lack of respect for authority (particularly generals, who gained a reputation for being aloof and absent from the front line, all the while sending battalions of men to death) and the enormous risk of fatality, there were few real dissenters in the British Army. There were 114,670 instances of desertion – just over 1.5 per cent of the total force mobilised from Britain and the Commonwealth. Of these, only 266 paid the ultimate penalty – execution. When this happened the telegram sent home to notify the family of death would not specify the cause; nor did the Commonwealth War Graves Commission record the reason. It was considered the most 'disgraceful death'. There were further executions, further ignominious fatalities, for cowardice (18), disobedience (5), striking or threatening a senior officer (5), sleeping at post (2), quitting post (7), shamefully casting away arms (2), mutiny (3) and murder (19). Men were shot by a firing party, which was usually made up of 12 men from their own unit.

The promise of leave, a few days when a soldier could get back home, was the chink of blue in his generally black skies. But leave could take a couple of years to come around and was granted only at the discretion of his officer, who might delay it if he needed all his men for an offensive. However, even if permission were given, getting home was in itself a challenge – the leave might be just for five days, and that included the

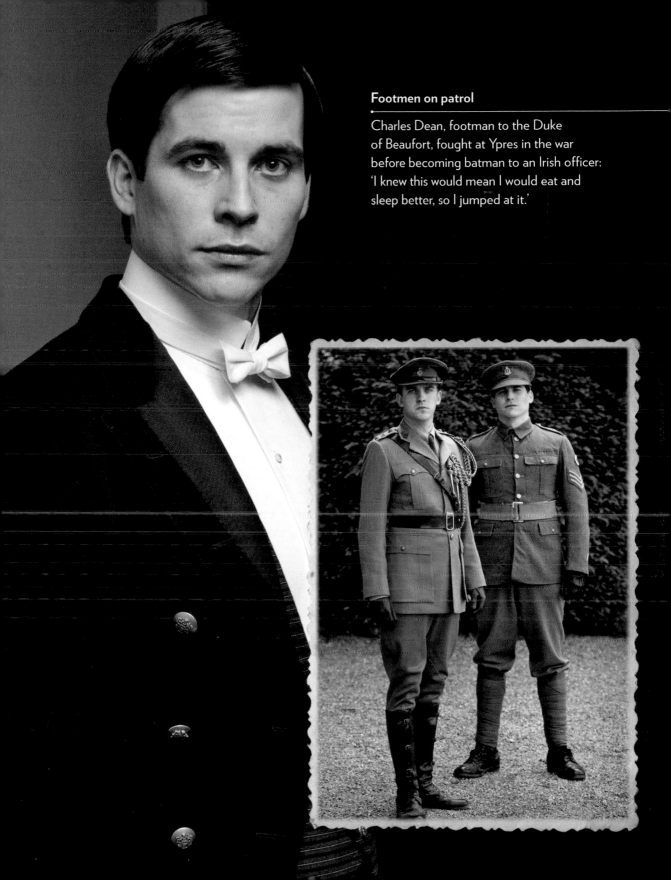

Footmen on patrol

Charles Dean, footman to the Duke
of Beaufort, fought at Ypres in the war
before becoming batman to an Irish officer:
'I knew this would mean I would eat and
sleep better, so I jumped at it.'

The effects of war

Alastair Bruce experienced a similar situation when he returned home from fighting in the Falklands War in 1982, which meant he was well able to brief the cast on how their characters would be feeling: 'The men came back changed – both mentally and physically they were unrecognisable. Both young men and women were affected. Women who had been getting ready for a life of tapestry and marriage were seeing their friends dying.' To help the cast better understand the atmosphere in which their characters would have lived, Alastair took to one side the male actors whose characters go to war, to discuss what their experiences would have been like. The men were then forbidden from discussing the details with the female actors, which helped to recreate the wall of secrecy that would have existed between their characters.

time spent travelling there and back, not so bad if you were stationed in the north of France and lived in the south of England, but pretty much hopeless if home was in Scotland, as the journey would eat into precious time off. Once back, the experience was often not the one they had dreamed of as they toiled in the trenches, since men found themselves alien to the life being lived at home, amongst people who knew little or nothing of the experiences they were enduring. Finding it too hard to explain what they had been through, most soldiers preferred to remain silent when they got home, their experiences remaining an enigma to even their closest friends and family.

For mothers, wives and sweethearts at home the sadness coursed through their veins, pumping hearts that beat anxiously to the rhythm of the postman's knock. A letter from the front was the most treasured possession, as heavily censored as it was – the men couldn't mention where

ROBERT

'The war is reaching its long fingers into Downton and scattering our chicks.'

they were or any details of military operations, although many devised codes to get around this. But the arrival of a letter was no guarantee that all was well: in the two or three days it had taken to reach them, the sender could have been killed. By far the most dreaded missive was a telegram from the War Office. If it didn't bring the tragic news that the soldier was dead, it might say that he was 'missing in action' – hardly words to raise hopes – or that he was 'wounded', which could mean anything from losing a leg to being poisoned by mustard gas.

For many women, work was a refuge from the interminable wait for news, but mothers and ladies of the upper classes who did not normally work, such as Cora, were not always able to find occupations to keep their minds off their men. While some worked in factories, on farms or as nurses, others were left to raise funds for the war effort or knit socks for soldiers. These were, of course, commendable occupations but the misery of long quiet hours in which to think must have been almost too much to bear.

Downton Abbey, situated in the north of England in the middle of the countryside, would not have suffered the frightening spectre of fighter planes overhead or the distant echo of bombshell. This meant that at the start of the war it was almost easy to forget that it was even happening. Almost, but not quite. The long lists of the dead that were printed daily in the newspapers and the knowledge that telegrams bearing bad news were arriving at the homes of friends and neighbours prevented complacency.

Despite this uncertainty, many pledged to 'carry on'; food was still relatively plentiful (rationing didn't come in until near the end of the war) and there was a spirited belief that keeping up appearances was a defiant show to the Germans, a way of letting them know that a war couldn't get the British down. The newspapers seemed to be inured to what was really going on at the front line, and even if they did know, their ability to report events was hampered by the necessity of shielding much of the horrific reality of war to ensure the nation's continued support. Lord Northcliffe's *Daily Mail* printed as much as it could about life on the front – even publishing letters sent home from the soldiers and passed on by their families after Kitchener threatened to shoot any reporter he found near the battle line. But all the newspapers faced a conundrum; to publish too much about the horrors of the war would damage morale and also possibly feed information to German spies, yet this war needed public support and without any real news terrible rumours spread, such as the one about Russian soldiers landing in Scotland with snow on their boots and marching to France. Eventually Kitchener allowed reporters onto the front line, but the best work newspapers did at that time was lobbying politicians rather than front line journalism.

EDITH

'Don't look so bewildered, it's simple. I will drive the tractor.'

Everyone was eager to maintain the standards of the past, even while they were desperately unsure about the future. But of course this meant that many returning soldiers felt even more disconnected when they got home. Others perhaps were grateful: they could believe the fight was worth it if their loved ones back home could still live their lives as before.

NATIONAL SERVICE
WOMEN'S LAND ARMY

GOD SPEED THE PLOUGH
AND THE WOMAN WHO DRIVES IT

SERIES W.B.

APPLY FOR ENROLMENT FORMS AT YOU[R]
EMPLOYMENT EX[CHANGE]

Jessica Brown-Findlay is Sybil

'The thing that shocked and attracted me to Sybil was that she's not like your usual period-drama romantic figure and I relate to her a little bit. When I was at school all the other girls would talk about boyfriends and tra-la-la, but I wanted to get on and do something. Sybil struck a chord with me. She was saying – I need to do something, but *what*? She feels the unjustness – her generation is being wiped out. In the first series she knows she wants to do something, in the second series she finds her purpose.'

As the war progressed, life on the home front, while obviously physically distant from the stench of blood and death of the front line, was nevertheless very much altered. Villages and towns were almost empty of young men; women filled their places and in doing so defined new roles for themselves. Those who had been fighting for suffrage – and even those who hadn't – were now actively able to demonstrate their ability to work and keep the country going. All this meant that come 1918, after the war had been won, the British Government argued that it was for this reason that they could at last grant women (over the age of 30) the vote.

SYBIL

'No. I don't mean selling programmes or finding prizes for the Tombola. I want to do a real job, real work.'

Many women found a sense of purpose during the war that their lives otherwise lacked (which is true for Sybil and Edith). Instead of sitting about waiting for marriage, they had work to do, which gave them independence and confidence. Learning to drive a tractor, as Edith does, let alone wearing trousers in order to do so, would have been unthinkable if there hadn't been a war on. As an aristocrat, it was extraordinary, though not unique, that Edith should choose to work on a farm; most went into nursing. They also worked in munitions factories, as bus conductors or train guards and on the docks. They were even found in the police force, as well as doing heavy work as blacksmiths and quarry workers, in gasworks and foundries, or lugging coal. Middle class women tended to take banking and clerical jobs in administration and education. No matter what they did, in all these jobs they were paid less than men, were classed as 'unskilled' and were largely forced to quit when the men came home.

While Edith's work is enjoyable, even fun, Sybil takes a much more challenging role as a nurse. While there were trained nurses working in the bigger city medical centres as well as in military and field hospitals, it soon became clear that there weren't enough of them to handle the huge numbers of wounded soldiers coming off the front line. Although more nurses were needed, there wasn't time to give them full training.

Help came in the form of the women who worked for the Voluntary Aid Detachment, or VADs, as they were known. They worked, unpaid, assisting the nurses at the hospitals – both permanent and makeshift. Some even said that it was the VADs that won the war. Their training was rudimentary – completed in just a few weeks to gain certificates in First Aid and Home Nursing from St John's Ambulance – and initially they were meant to perform only light duties such as serve tea, change bedsheets and sterilise equipment. But it wasn't long before they were also rushing to help the doctors, perhaps by holding down quivering limbs as amputees had their wounds dressed. They learnt on the job, having to think quickly on their aching, tired feet.

As a voluntary commission, the VADs tended to be middle- and upper-class women, like Sybil, as they were the only ones who could afford to work for no pay. (Board and lodging would be paid for, but unless you were in a military hospital, which most were not, there were no wages at all.) This meant that many of these women were unprepared for the harsh reality of coping with a constant stream of desperately ill and injured soldiers. Vera Brittain was an upper-middle-class Oxford undergraduate who could not boil an egg when she began ('I imagined that I had to bring the saucepan to the boil, then turn off the gas and allow the egg to lie for three minutes in the cooling water'), but she noticed that the professional nurses admired her enthusiasm for even the most revolting of tasks. Perhaps this admiration stemmed from the fact that most of the local VADs 'came to the hospital expecting to hold the patients' hands and smooth their pillows while the regular nurses fetched and carried everything that looked or smelt disagreeable.'

While Sybil may have encountered some of the more gruesome aspects of nursing during her training at a large hospital in York, her work at Downton Abbey while it was a convalescent home would have been less frantic and shocking. This is not to say it would have been easy, as there would still have been amputations to dress, and the intimate ablutions of men to attend to. Unmarried women like Sybil, brought up to know nothing of men other than as they were fully dressed in public, gained an education that set them apart from their sisters. Sybil, like most women of her class, would never have even been in the presence of a man without a chaperone. War soon changed that. 'Short of actually going to bed with them,' wrote Vera Brittain, 'there was hardly an intimate service that I did not perform for one or another in the course of four years.'

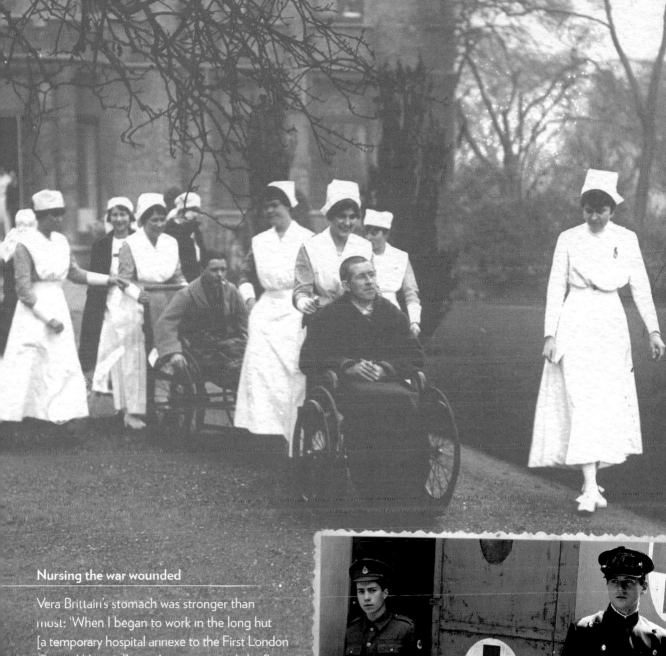

Nursing the war wounded

Vera Brittain's stomach was stronger than most: 'When I began to work in the long hut [a temporary hospital annexe to the First London General Hospital], my duties consisted chiefly in preparing dressing-trays and supporting limbs – a task which the orderlies seldom undertook because they were so quickly upset by the butcher's-shop appearance of the uncovered wounds. Soon after I arrived I saw one of them, who was holding a basin, faint right on top of the patient.'

One of the most terrible afflictions encountered during the war, which had never been known before, was shellshock. Usually triggered by nearness to a shell explosion, it was a psychological condition that manifested itself in many and varying ways, making an understanding of the condition, let alone treatment, difficult. Men suffering from shell shock were essentially having a nervous breakdown. They could, however, still function and talk normally, so this meant that many people were not as sympathetic towards them as they might have been.

VIOLET, THE DOWAGER COUNTESS

'Oh really, it's like living in a second-rate hotel, where the guests keep arriving and no-one seems to leave.'

More physically shocking to witness were the effects of mustard gas. While tear gas and chlorine gas had been deployed earlier in the war – the first time chemical warfare had been used – they were soon overshadowed by the horrors of mustard gas. While not always fatal, its effects were exceptionally nasty. Victims suffered blistering skin, temporary or permanent blindness, internal and external bleeding, vomiting and an attack on the bronchial tubes, stripping them of the mucous membrane, which was extremely painful.

In the face of the courage shown by their comrades, perhaps the most shocking – if nonetheless understandable – injury was the self-inflicted one. Known as a 'Blighty', it was a wound serious enough to get you sent home, but not so serious as to cause a handicap. Harder still to look at were the numerous amputees, their limbs often blown away by an explosion, or sawn off near the battlefields to rescue quickly what was left of a wounded arm or leg that had turned septic. Trench foot was also a dreadful problem in the early years of the war; soldiers who had been standing for days on end in waterlogged trenches without taking off their shoes and socks went numb below the ankle and risked their feet becoming gangrenous and needing amputation. The solution was almost pathetically simple: men had to dry their feet and change their socks at least twice a day, under orders.

War ended on the eleventh hour of the eleventh of November 1918. By that time more than nine million people around the world had been killed in the conflict. Of these, 989,075 were British, with another 2,121,906 wounded. Just over six per cent of the population was either injured or dead. Of those who returned alive, many were unfit for work. They may have looked physically able but if suffering from shellshock, they found it almost impossible to live easily. Many, many others had been through experiences so devastating and alien to life back home that they had enormous difficulty in adjusting. Nor did they all return to a hero's welcome. It was a common sight to see a former war soldier begging on the streets, his injuries – whether physical or mental – prohibiting him from finding work. People were desperate to forget the war and just get back to normal, but things could never be the same again. Families had lost their sons, towns had lost their workforce, children had lost their fathers. One mother from Watford lost four of her five sons, dying herself of heartbreak not long after. Nor was she exceptional in her loss. When the 'Unknown Warrior' was buried at Westminster Abbey in a state ceremony at which the King placed a wreath on the coffin, the guests of honour were 100 women who had lost their husbands and all their sons to the war.

SYBIL

'Sometimes it feels as if all the men I ever danced with are dead.'

The war was over, but normality was still some distance off. The previous ebullience of *la belle époque* at the turn of the century, with Britain's party-loving King Edward VII and the marvels of modern inventions such as the telephone and airplane that had created the feverish excitement of a new century, had been blown away. Matthew and his comrades would return – if they returned at all – never to be the same again. Wounded men who faced their remaining years in either a wheelchair or on crutches had lost their independence and their livelihoods.

Sybil had experienced a side of life that women of her class had almost never seen – it could only leave her affected in untold ways, changing the face of her previously ordained future. Edith, whose chance of marriage had been slimmer than her sisters before the war, now had an even narrower field to choose from – and after what she had been through in the war, quiet domesticity might not hold quite the same appeal any more.

Spanish 'Flu

In October 1918, just as the war was ending and Britain was hoping to get back to some sort of ordinariness, the Spanish 'Flu struck. An epic natural disaster, it swept around the world between June 1917 and December 1920, killing an estimated 50 million people. In Britain, as many as 250,000 died from the pandemic. Unusually, this strain of influenza was most deadly for young adults, people aged between 20 and 40 years old, and it could kill within hours of striking its victim.

KEEP YOUR BED ROOM WINDOWS OPEN!

PREVENT INFLUENZA- PNEUMONIA- TUBERCULOSIS

FOR FURTHER PRINTED DIRECTIONS, CONSULT

ANTI-TUBERCULOSIS LEAGUE OR BOARD OF HEALTH

ALLIES' DRASTIC ARMISTICE TERMS TO HUNS

The Daily Mirror

CERTIFIED CIRCULATION LARGER THAN THAT OF ANY OTHER DAILY PICTURE PAPER

No. 4,696.   Registered at the G.P.O. as a Newspaper.   **TUESDAY, NOVEMBER 12, 1918.**   One Penny.

HOW LONDON HAILED THE END OF WAR

The King and Queen appeared on the balcony at Buckingham Palace to acknowledge the cheers of the crowd that gathered to congratulate their Majesties on the victory.

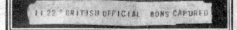

Home on short leave, but now safe for always from the dangers of Hun bullet and steel.

How news of the armistice signature came over the wire to the newspaper offices. A facsimile of it as automatically printed on the tape machine. The cheers which greeted it were the first to be raised.

An historic message as it came over the wire. It is dramatic that the last British war communiqué should proclaim our forces at Mons.

"Now entitled to rejoice" and doing it. Daddy has beaten the Huns and is coming home.

Nothing gave greater satisfaction to all of us than the news that the cessation of hostilities found the British armies once more in possession of Mons, where the immortal

"Contemptibles" first taught the Huns what British valour and steadfastness could do. They left the town as defenders of a forlorn hope; they re-entered it conquerors indeed.

Servants like Thomas who had had a brief period of authority would find it difficult to adjust to the old ways again – if, indeed, they could at all. His colleagues would have to realign their roles once more: women had taken on some of the men's tasks and could be reluctant to hand them back. Nor was replacing missing staff simple when so many had been either killed or experienced a life that meant they were no longer content to work as servants but wanted instead the freedom of living in towns and better pay for factory or secretarial work. Besides, many men had endured the consequences of incompetence by generals, let alone the fact of their 'King and country' sending them to war, and there was less respect for authority, less belief in government propaganda.

LORD GRANTHAM

'We've dreamed a dream, my dear, but now it's over. The world was in a dream before the war but now it's woken up and said goodbye to it. And so must we.'

Food prices had increased hugely over the war years and essentials such as meat, bacon, butter and jam were now rationed. The country was in debt thanks to the enormous cost of the war and the landowners found themselves hit with big taxes. Downton Abbey and other similar houses, many of which would have transformed themselves into convalescent homes or hospitals (like Highclere) during the war, now had to consider carefully whether they could continue to operate as before.

The Great War did not leave a single person unscathed. Those who survived the front may have been alive but they could never be the same again. Those who had stayed at home had endured heartache and sadness as they watched their brave young men go, and most of them never return. Neither privilege nor riches could protect anyone from the brutality that those years wrought upon them. Downton Abbey is a house that has stood for hundreds of years, but its walls were not thick enough to shield its inhabitants from the brutality of the outside world. And yet, life did go on.

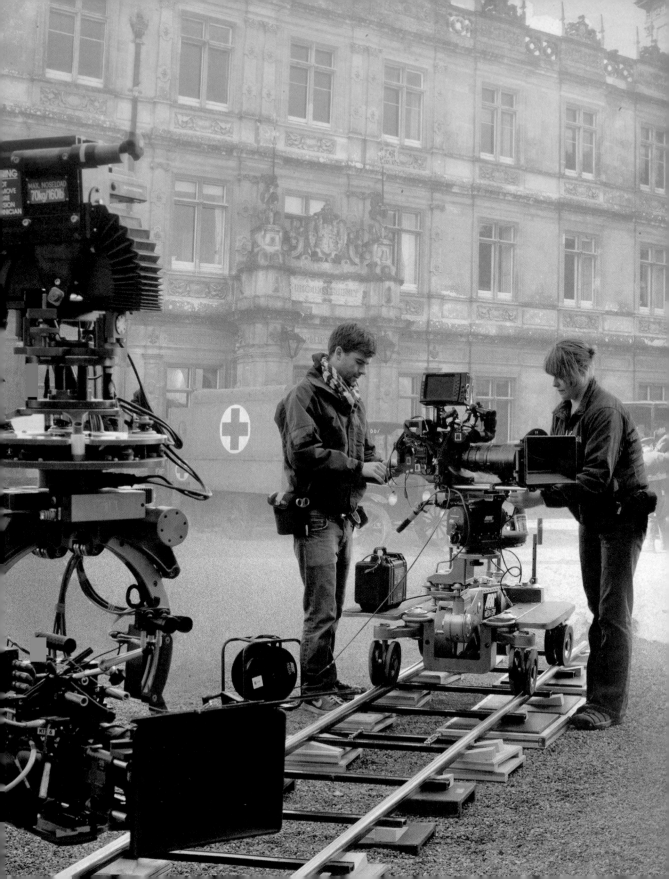

Behind the Scenes

CHAPTER NINE

Daisy comes up the grim kitchen staircase and pushes open the door. Beyond is a different world, with the light from a high glass dome playing on pictures in gilt frames, on Turkish carpets and the gleaming floor. In a long, tracking shot, we follow her as she crosses the great hall into the marble-floored entrance hall.

*T*he world of Downton Abbey is thoroughly embedded in the reality of life in Britain a hundred years ago. But for all that is real about it, the compelling fact is that *every single* element you watch on screen is a figment of imagination. The script was brought to life by a dedicated production team and a cast of actors, but the origin of its existence lies in a small restaurant in London's Belgravia, where Gareth Neame and Julian Fellowes met one night for supper.

Gareth, managing director of independent production company Carnival Films, and Julian were discussing a project they had that wasn't working, which they decided to set aside for a bit. Then Gareth asked Julian if he might ever be persuaded to write a television series that revisited his Oscar-winning *Gosford Park* territory. 'I thought that as an episodic serial you'd have a timescale to get right inside the lives of everyone above and below stairs, in a way that you can't in a film. I knew it would play to the strengths of television and had a hunch it would be very popular. With Julian writing it, I knew it would be authentic,' says Gareth.

At first Julian was unsure: 'I replied that it would be like trying to make lightning strike in the same place twice,' he says. Nevertheless, 'it planted a seed.' Around that time, Julian was reading a book about American heiresses who came to Britain in the late 1800s and he began to wonder what it would be like to come from, say, Milwaukee, and become part of the British aristocracy. Thus the idea for Cora was born. Not long after that meeting, Julian produced a 'thought bible', which contained descriptions of all the characters, as well as the Crawley dilemma of the great estate with no heir.

All-day dining

A dining scene may last only a few minutes, but it can take between 10 and 12 hours to film. This is because the director needs to shoot each actor and that can mean three or four takes per person. Dan Stevens says he quickly learned not to eat during these scenes: 'If you decide you're going to eat, say, five mouthfuls of chicken, then by the end of the day you've had about 70 and it's cold and congealed.'

Zoe Boyle is Lavinia

When filming at Highclere, actress Zoe Boyle, who plays Lavinia Swire, says it is similar to

Twelfth Night? Or What You Will...

When Laura Carmichael auditioned for the part of Edith, she was working as a doctor's receptionist between theatre jobs. Laura was waiting to hear whether she had a part in a production of *Twelfth Night* that was going to Dubai, but had to decline it before she even knew if she'd got *Downton Abbey*. 'My friends were saying I had better be prepared for the worst, which was a bit worrying! But luckily on the Monday I had a callback for *Downton Abbey* and by Thursday I'd got the job.'

Dan Stevens is Matthew

'We had to reshoot a scene, as I hadn't stood up when Violet came into the room. Alastair Bruce wasn't there that day unfortunately! I had to learn to doff my hat any time a woman walks past. Even if it's not the full doff, there has to be a little raise. We worked hard on my doff.'

Julian set the series in 1912 because it was a time when England was 'teetering on the brink. Downton Abbey seems so secure, it's as if the way of life it represents will last for ever. But in fact it won't. It would be less than ten years before the First World War and the Jazz Age had ripped every certainty to shreds.' The year is also interesting because, as Julian remarks: 'This fascinating period is the beginning of the modern era as we know it. There are no high-bosomed ladies skipping down the stairs to collect a letter as you'd get in a Jane Austen novel – people had cars, electricity and telephones. They had begun to commute on the Underground, and families were getting pensions and mortgages. There is so much we can relate to.'

PENELOPE WILTON (ISOBEL CRAWLEY)

'At Highclere you feel like a visitor. It helps because as
a character, she thinks – how on earth is my son going
to manage this? He hasn't been brought up to it,
it's been forced upon him.'

Gareth knew he wanted to take the series to ITV: 'The ITV I had grown up with had produced some big, classy dramas – *The Jewel In The Crown*, *Brideshead Revisited* – and I saw no reason for those days to be over. Plus, I felt that with ITV we could make a bigger noise and reach a broader audience. That was what I hoped would happen and it did! It exceeded even my expectations.'

Once the series had been given the green light, in the summer of 2009, Gareth brought on board producer Nigel Marchant, series producer Liz Trubridge and production designer Donal Woods. Now they could start to put together the nuts and bolts of making the show. First off they had to cast the principal character in the series: the house itself. Julian had already suggested Highclere Castle, in Berkshire, which was a location he had originally thought of for *Gosford Park* but the film's director, Robert Altman, had felt it was too far from London, as he wanted everyone to sleep in their own beds at night. Gareth and Donal loved Highclere, but it was only after they had spent six months travelling around the country and looking at other houses that they finally agreed on the stately home. 'We looked at around 30 houses,' says Donal.

The below stairs set

The 'below stairs' of Downton is filmed on a carefully designed set at Ealing Studios in London. The set was developed from detailed plans and even an intricate scale model, shown above. The complete set took five weeks of pre-build preparation – with some elements being made off-site – and 14 weeks to construct in situ. About 25 people worked on the build, including five painters and around 14 chippies. All the props are hired from specialist companies.

The bell board

The names of all the upstairs rooms are on the bell board in the servants' hall: the bedrooms – Portico, Arundel, Queen Caroline, Mercia, East Anglia, Grantham, Stanhope, York, Ripon, Wetherby – as well as the dining room, morning room, library, small library, saloon, front door, back door, study, drawing room and west room.

Brian Percival, director

'Sophie [McShera, who plays Daisy] said to me one day, "We never get to see the house", and it suddenly dawned on me that the set was a carbon copy of what went on in history. A number of actors never went to the other location – it was art imitating life!'

'But they were all either too big or not big enough.' 'Every house had something,' says Gareth. 'But Highclere was the only one to join all the dots.' They also wanted to demonstrate through the house that this series was set in a different era to the more usual period dramas. This meant that creamy Georgian houses with stucco fronts and Palladian columns were out. 'Highclere Castle was just right because its stone is similar to what you would find in Leeds or York, and the Charles Barry architecture typifies the late- to mid-Victorian look,' says Donal.

ROB JAMES-COLLIER (THOMAS)

'Below stairs I can relax a bit more in terms of posture and the way I speak. It's like putting on a telephone voice, when above stairs. It's definitely more measured and you just naturally want to adopt the postures.'

Nor did Highclere Castle look right from the outside only. The rooms were all wonderfully equipped to tell the story of a family with an ancient earldom because that is exactly what they were already doing in every portrait, every book and every piece of furniture. Essentially, the history of the Carnarvons was borrowed and transferred to the Granthams. So very little in the way of props had to be imported to create the right feel for the period. 'We brought in a lot of the things that were for personal use,' says Donal. 'The furniture was changed around and we put in potted palms – they were all the rage then.' Although Art Nouveau was fashionable at that time, 'it bypassed the aristocracy,' says Donal. 'The only time you see it in *Downton Abbey* is for the brief scene in Episode One of the first series when we see the Crawleys in their Manchester house. They would have had "trendy" furniture.'

Rose Leslie, who plays housemaid Gwen, was in awe of the grandeur at Highclere: 'On my first day I looked up and I had to let my neck go completely to be able to see all the way to the top.'

Like most great houses today, however, while the public rooms are beautifully maintained, the servants' quarters no longer exist in their original state. So for the scenes 'below stairs' Donal had to design an entire floor of servants' quarters, and their attic bedrooms, to be built and filmed at Ealing Studios – 60 miles away. This means that scenes

Getting the right view

Different camera work was done for above and below stairs – while upstairs filming tended to be smooth, for the below stairs scenes, the director used handheld cameras more frequently. 'It's more edgy and truthful below stairs in some ways,' says first series director Brian Percival. 'We are observing these characters, it's not a photo opportunity.'

The kitchen

The look of the kitchen was 'stolen from our endless trips to country houses,' says Donal. 'Harewood House in Leeds was a big influence.' Most kitchens were double-storey compared to the other rooms in the basement, built on one side of the house, with small, high windows. The walls are painted in Farrow & Ball colours – French Grey and Cat's Paw on the walls, Buff on the cupboards. The sinks are brown earthenware and were found in a reclamation yard in Suffolk. Smith Carbon disinfectant powder sits by the taps. None of the cupboard doors or drawers open, but there is running water for the sink and two of the hot plates on the range work. There are real Indian flagstones on the floor – a common feature of country house kitchens. Scuffs are painted on but the set takes a bit of bashing during filming – normally this would be a problem, but on a set like this, the more wear it has, the better it looks.

Setting the scene

When it came to kitchen scenes, the stand-by art director, Philippa Broadhurst, used detailed notes she had taken from various references, including the 1912 *Edinburgh Cookbook for Smart Houses*, to get ideas for background activities.

The range

The range was built by the kitchen firm Cutler & Gross, using a combination of three different ranges. It was designed to be the right size for the house and the number of people it would have been catering for – not just the family, but all the servants, too. On top of the range is a large copper vat with a tap that supplied constant hot water.

The table

This was made for the set using real timber, which was then wire-wooled, brushed, bleached, scorched, stained and sanded. Bowls, knives and baking tins are stacked beneath the table on a lower tier.

Joanne Froggatt is Anna

'Alastair Bruce taught me how to make a bed properly. You lay the sheet out, then you fold the corners as if you were wrapping a present and tuck them back under the mattress. Then the blankets and the coverspread. Oh! But before all that you put the bolster ... No, the sheet, then the bolster. Or is it the bolster and then an oversheet on that? It's complicated! I'm constantly asking Alastair questions.'

shot above and below stairs are filmed two weeks apart, which made for some interesting continuity issues. For example, Thomas might be filmed leaving the kitchen with a plate of food for upstairs and would then appear two weeks later in the dining room!

For Jessica Brown-Findlay (Sybil), the house helped her understand her own character. 'Alastair Bruce gave us a talk before filming and he said the big storyline is this house. It's where your family have lived for generations, it's *why* you're there. It's not about demonstrating how rich you are, it's about preserving it and valuing it. He said it all very well but it was only when I first drove up and saw this looming house and inside with the great rooms that I understood. I could see why you would be so protective.' The scale had another unexpected side-effect: 'I found myself speaking louder in the rooms because they were so much bigger. You felt "I'm right" just because you were someone whose opinions would be heard.'

JOANNE FROGGATT (ANNA)

'As a character I'd love to see Anna marry and live happily ever after, but as an actress I hope she doesn't!'

On location at Ealing Studios in West London (the world's oldest working film studio and home of the Ealing Comedies), the atmosphere is more workmanlike. Not least because this is where the art department and production offices are based for the duration of the shoot. But the really telling factor is that whereas in Highclere the cameras move about in rooms that have stood for hundreds of years, at Ealing Studios everything from the walls to the smallest prop has to be built, made or hired.

Donal decided to keep the colours of the servants' quarters fairly monochromatic, using warm greys, creams and blacks from the Farrow & Ball paint range. 'Nothing jarred. Even the props and their uniforms had those muted colours,' says Donal. 'The idea was that when you went through the green baize door upstairs you'd be hit with a blaze of colour, almost like a slap in the face.'

As well as the kitchen, servants' hall, Carson's pantry, Mrs Hughes' sitting-room and the servants' bedrooms, they also built Mary's bedroom and Robert's dressing room at Ealing Studios. 'We built two doors for

Making yourself heard

Penny Dyer, dialogue coach: 'The real difference in speech with a period piece is not so much the pronunciation of the words but that the height of the ceilings and the size of the rooms affect the voice. For example, those who work below stairs probably grew up with large families in a cramped household, scrabbling for space beneath low ceilings, so their sound is pushed sideways.' This would mean those above stairs would naturally project their voices to fill larger rooms.

every room, so that in the filming there would be a fluid camera roll, following one person out and another in,' says Donal.

'The downstairs set had to feel underground – it's the factory end of a beautiful house. It needs to be abuzz with activity, with the kitchen steaming and hot, the walls stuffed with what-not and people dragging things around. It's not a National Trust picture of serenity.'

Filming in two different locations made for two very different atmospheres. For one thing, many of the 'above stairs' characters did little filming at Ealing Studios and vice versa. Only a few actors, such as Jim Carter (Carson) and Brendan Coyle (Bates), travelled frequently between the two, although everybody got a chance to 'see how the other half lives.' Joanne Froggatt (Anna), says of the experience: 'It's a real pleasure filming in both locations – I really enjoy it, I like change anyway in my life and to do different things. When the sun is shining, Highclere is a gorgeous place to work and the house is stunning. But at Ealing, there's real history and the set is amazing – it's huge! I've never worked on a set of that quality and size before. Also, that weather element isn't there.' Filming at Highclere can be a cold experience, as the house stands on a hill. The views are beautiful but the wind makes even a mild day chilly, so the actresses had to wear legwarmers beneath their dresses.

For Siobhan Finneran, as O'Brien, Ealing Studios was the best place to be: 'I loved being at Highclere, it's an amazing place, but I just loved all the scenes around the table in the servants' hall. Because we all get on very well there's such a good atmosphere there.'

As well as Highclere and Ealing Studios, the entire unit would have to move to film scenes that took place outside 'Downton Abbey' itself. The village scenes were filmed in Bampton, Oxfordshire. The Dower House is Byfleet Manor, a very pretty Wren house. 'We wanted to deliberately pull Violet back into that Georgian world,' says Donal. The exterior of the Crawley house is one that sits in Bampton village, but the interiors were shot in Beaconsfield, in a Georgian house called Hall Place. For the war scenes, Matthew's dugout was recreated at Ealing Studios but the trenches were filmed in Ackenham, Ipswich, a location which has been specially built for First and Second World War recreations.

Liz Trubridge, series producer, started working on *Downton Abbey* when it was first commissioned and hasn't stopped since – when editing for the US transmissions had finished, she immediately began work on

Graphic Props

Lucy Spofforth is the assistant art director and she is in charge of all the graphics – anything that is printed that appears on the programme, from a packet of biscuits to a letter or a painted sign. Originals are sourced as often as possible, but they can look too old, so Lucy remakes things like beer labels. The Downton crest was created in order to be printed on menus, calling cards and writing paper. It features an earl's coronet over two Gs intertwined. It is deliberately both austere and delicate.

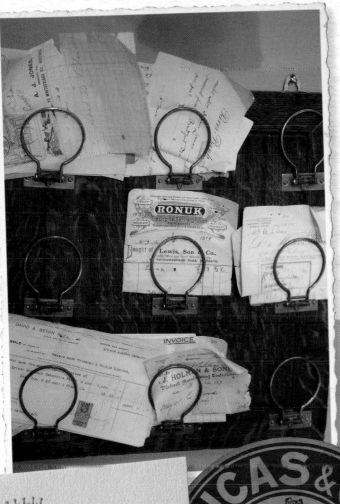

Donal Woods, production designer

'Officer's quarters were 4.25m (14ft) square
for four of them, two on and two off, with
their servants next door. It would also be
used as a communications post. We used
upturned turf on the floor and put mould on
all the wood. They were semi-underground
and had that damp stickiness. The dugouts
were in a constant state of repair because of
the shelling. Inside, everyone had standard
issue army equipment, but we also found
things that they would have taken as small
mementoes from home – pictures of their
rugby teams or sporting trophies.'

Rosalind Ebbutt – costume designer and specialist in military uniforms

'I asked if we could film the dugout scenes after the trenches, as we'd need to know what colour the mud was. We brought back big buckets of mud to get it right. We gave them silk ski thermal underwear, socks and pants, then thick vests, towelling sports sock and another pair of thermal socks so that the actors were OK – not too cold.'

Getting the right look

The real task came with the war scenes. 'I'm the wartime blood and guts girl,' says Anne 'Nosh' Oldham, who has done the make-up for *Dunkirk* and *Welcome to Sarajevo*, so she rose to the challenge with relish. For one character who was suffering from poison gas blindness, they gave him lenses that covered the entire eye to make them look 'cloudy' with burst blood vessels. 'The skin blisters are surprisingly easy to do. You apply silicone with a gun, then mould it into shape before putting a thin wash of colour over it, a little red.'

Real amputees play the men wounded in battle, but Nosh needed to create bloody stumps. 'We got the best effect with apples, using mushrooms for the exposed bone. Soft dried fruit was the best for the layer of fat around the "bone" and it soaked up the blood beautifully. We held it all together with gelatine and stuck it on a popsock so the men didn't have to have it on all day but could just put it on when needed.'

Liz Trubridge, Series Producer

'When filming in the trenches, Julian Fellowes was walking through the set between takes when he suddenly fell down flat in the mud. He was a very good sport about it – after using the cameraman's cleaning cloths to wipe off his face.'

Convalescing officers' dormitory

This is the drawing room, where the family normally retires for their coffee after dinner. The paintings, chandelier and larger pieces of furniture (the piano is hidden beneath a cotton cover) all belong to Highclere Castle. The large rug is hired, however, as Highclere's is too modern.

There are extra grey woollen blankets and sheets for the nurses to carry around. Various props were brought in just for the actors to have in their hands when they needed to look busy – a tray of glasses and a book trolley, for example. There's an oil lamp here in case the electricity generator breaks down. It was run like a hospital – at night the officers had to go to sleep when matron decided it was time for 'lights out'.

Props

The Campaign wash-stands are what would be used in a field hospital or for an army on the move.

Historical detail

The beds are the same ones seen in Dr Clarkson's local college hospital, as well as in some scenes shot at Leeds Infirmary but there they have different covers. The beds are originals as are the covers, hired from a company that specialises in period fabrics – which may have originally come from a naval hospital, as there are small anchors sewn on the corners.

Susannah Buxton, costume designer

'You have to consider the scenes as a whole with everything interacting on screen together, like a painting. Donal will tell me the overall colour of a room and from there I look for the pieces. For the second series, I needed to have ready three evening dresses [for each actress], with two finished in time for filming, plus their basic wardrobe including nightgowns and teagowns.'

Costume fittings

For the first meeting with an actor, Susannah pulls together a rail of clothes. 'I have all the different relevant skirt shapes and jacket shapes – we have to see what looks good on a particular actor. The first fitting is about colour and shape. I photograph anything that works and use it for ideas. If anything is too tricky to find, I make it. For this series, with 18 people changing all the time, it's incredibly complicated. We have seven weeks prep before filming begins and that's just enough time to get together the costumes for the first two episodes.'

All the actresses wear plain, nude-coloured, cling-resistant slips from Marks & Spencer under their dresses and they love them so much they have become addicted to wearing them off-set too.

the second series. 'From the moment it gets the green light, we start discussing storylines, mapping out the story arc and working out roughly what will happen, although it does inevitably change,' says Liz. Although he had written novels and film scripts, as well as the book for the international stage musical *Mary Poppins*, Julian had only adapted novels for television before, so this was new territory. The best discovery for him was that during filming the characters started to take on their own lives and he could write accordingly. 'For example in the first episode we'd already got O'Brien and Thomas, but their parts were certainly elaborated after the read through and from then on. Because of their performances, they came more and more to the front,' says Julian.

Susannah Buxton has worked on Series One and Two as costume designer, with Rosalind Ebbutt joining from Episode Three of the second series. During the weeks before filming, Susannah works from an office at Cosprop, the second biggest costume house in London. 'I've also been to source things in Madrid, Spain. We have workrooms upstairs at Cosprop and another small one at Ealing Studios because it's a non-stop sewing show,' Susannah explains. The costumes are produced in three different ways: hired, made and bought. 'I'll find bits and pieces in the costume house,' says Susannah. 'I might find a bodice and it will be the wrong colour, but something in the shape might work. You can't just look at a picture and think, "Yes, I'll use it." And in the same way that the people of that time would re-use pieces for themselves, we re-use them in the show. For example, Lady Edith's jacket that she wears down on the farm for Series Two was one of her smart jackets from the first series.'

Anne 'Nosh' Oldham is the hair and make-up designer for both series of *Downton Abbey*. The challenge for Nosh is that no one can look as if they are wearing make-up. 'At that time, only whorish girls and actresses wore blusher and that sort of thing,' says Nosh. Lesley Nicol, as Mrs Patmore, is the only actress in the ensemble who doesn't wear any make-up at all, apart from some special effects: 'We've given her burn marks on her arms from where she would have caught them taking things in and out of the oven over the years.'

As O'Brien, Siobhan Finneran is almost unrecognisable. Her transformation 'takes about 50 minutes. When Siobhan filmed Series One, she'd just been shooting *Benidorm* and her hair was very blonde. So I put it in a ponytail and switched it up – the false fringe covered the blonde at the front. It's a combination of wanting to use the actress's own hair

Perfect hair

Maggie Smith as Violet is 'very va-va voom' says Nosh, 'but as she doesn't like to be in the chair for long, her wig is prepared beforehand so it can be put on like a hat. All the wigs are tailormade for the actresses, but Maggie has her own wigmaker, Peter Owen, who is not only one of the best there is but he has always worked with her so knows exactly what will be right.'

The secret of slick hair

'We tried to put Brilliantine in Jim Carter's hair, but he said he kept sticking to his pillow at night and his poor wife couldn't get the stuff off their sheets! So we went back to Kiehl's hair products.'

but needing to cover up blonde. We use as much of their own hair as possible. Then it was just a bit of base and lip colour. We dye all the actress's eyelashes,' explains Nosh.

Elizabeth McGovern spends a little under an hour-and-a-half in the make-up chair to become Cora. 'She doesn't mind, she likes to look gorgeous and when she leaves the chair she feels absolutely perfect,' says Nosh. 'For her we draw a little onto her eyebrows, she has a tiny bit of eyeliner and some false eyelashes on the outside edges. We mix two bases – we use Armani and Chanel for all the actresses – which are translucent but give luminosity. We don't put it on all over, just where it's needed. If you don't put base on the eyelids, to leave a natural pinkness around the eyes, it makes it look as if you're not wearing any at all. We also add a bit of blusher and some lip colour – that's probably the only thing you can see on Cora. For her hair, the centre and parting is her own, the rest is a piece added on, which gives her width.'

Actors were reminded not to say 'nee-ther'
or 'ee-ther' but 'nye-ther' and 'eye-ther'. The former
only came into use after the Second World War when the
American soldiers came to Britain.

Michelle Dockery as Mary has similar make-up – the girls all have some base and a few false eyelashes – and only a small piece of false hair added in. Laura Carmichael as Edith has her hair bobbed and a piece added to the back. Jessica Brown-Findlay as Sybil has a deliberately dressed-down look this series: 'When she came back from doing her first Season [in Series One] we had her with her hair up – it signifies that a girl is ready for marriage. But for the dinner scenes in Series Two we keep it pretty simple – she doesn't have much time to do anything to her hair after working as a nurse all day.'

Julian originally wrote the character of Lavinia Swire as a 'peaches and cream' blonde, but when Nosh met the actress playing her, Zoe Boyle, 'I saw she has the most wonderful skin tone that goes with her reddish hair beautifully – it would have looked all wrong with blonde. So I asked Julian if we could possibly reconsider her colouring and luckily he agreed. She wears a big piece on the back, making it look very elaborate.'

The Oracle

Alastair Bruce was probably the most popular man on set. He quickly became known for providing the answers not just to history questions but 'life, love and everything' says Rob James-Collier (Thomas). Nicknames he acquired included 'The Oracle', 'Yoda', 'Big Al' and even 'God'. Allen Leach (Branson) probably did the best deal: 'Every day I'd ask him to tell me something I didn't know and in return I'd give him a racing tip.'

Setting up for a fall

When Brendan Coyle (Bates) had to fall in the gravel in the first series, after O'Brien trips him up, it took several takes: 'I must have done it 18 times and by the end I was wounded! I wore knee pads and a torso shield, but when you fall you have to really commit to falling. Metaphorically and physically he had to fall flat on his face, it had to be humiliating.'

The village – at Bampton, Oxfordshire

'We filmed in the village of Bampton, which was so friendly and all the people there put up with an awful lot. Not very long before we were due to start filming there, the wall in the main street collapsed. So our amazing art department went and built the wall back up again!' Liz recalls.

Dan Stevens is Matthew

'It took a while to shoot the scene by the coconut stall at the fun fair, so Michelle (Mary) and I had a competition. I think she beat me 10-1 – she was uncannily good. The crew were very disappointed in me. To be beaten by a woman is bad enough, but one in Edwardian dress is really highlighting something.'

Contemporary clashes

A matter of days before filming started a huge amount of scaffolding went up around the church at one end of the village. It was due to come down two days after filming was scheduled to finish. Rather than rely on post-production to delete it, the director, Brian Percival, carefully shot around it so that it was never seen onscreen.

'The progression from 1914 to 1916 is slight because during the war everything changes but fashion,' says Nosh. 'I've changed the shape of the girls' hair slightly and simplified things a bit because they are more preoccupied this time, Sybil with her nursing and Edith with her farmwork. They would have been concentrating on other things than getting their hair done. Also, in this series Mary is more of a young woman than a girl.'

All the music heard throughout the series is composed by John Lunn. John starts to put the music together only once the programme has been finally edited: 'You need the music to take you through the scenes, so the timing is very important. I'm a big advocate of using music to do something that's not on the screen or in the dialogue.' It was only after John had scored the music for the first episode that the theme tune itself emerged: 'In the opening episode there's a scene where we follow Daisy as she goes through the house and that's where most of the music comes from.' John chose not to particularly reference music from that time as 'a lot of the popular music then was unrelentingly happy'. Once the music has been written, it is recorded in blocks of two episodes at London's famous Abbey Road Studios, using an orchestra composed mainly of string instruments and the cor anglais, a wind instrument.

Filmed in the first half of 2010, the show at that point was an unknown entity to anyone outside the production; nobody knew whether it would be a success or not. 'The experience of making the show was very enjoyable because it went so smoothly and was so straightforward,' says Gareth 'I almost worried! But we had brilliant scripts, great key production team and great actors. When we came to the edit, I really felt it was good, a very polished piece. Of course, you have no idea until you show people. We showed it to the press first in September of that year and that generated enormous buzz. We also did a gala screening before the first episode went out and that got a very strong reaction. But once it went out on TV, it was extraordinary. I've never known anything like it. To debut well and go up and up [in the viewing figures] was exceptional. It's very rare for a TV show to step out of the box and become part of the national conversation.'

The first episode, screened on 26 September 2010, had viewing figures of nine million. By the time of the final episode, on 7 November, 12.8 million were watching. The onslaught of the *Downton Abbey* effect was palpable and it has hardly let up since.

CAST LIST

Robert Bathurst	—	Sir Anthony Strallan
Samantha Bond	—	Lady Rosamund Painswick
Hugh Bonneville	—	Robert Crawley, Earl of Grantham
Zoe Boyle	—	Lavinia Swire
Jessica Brown Findlay	—	Lady Sybil Crawley
Clare Calbraith	—	Jane Moorsum
Laura Carmichael	—	Lady Edith Crawley
Jim Carter	—	Charles Carson
Charlie Cox	—	Duke of Crowborough
Jonathan Coy	—	George Murray
Brendan Coyle	—	John Bates
Michelle Dockery	—	Lady Mary Crawley
Kevin Doyle	—	Alfred Molesley
Maria Doyle Kennedy	—	Vera Bates
Siobhan Finneran	—	Sarah O'Brien
Joanne Froggatt	—	Anna Smith
Iain Glen	—	Sir Richard Carlisle
Thomas Howes	—	William Mason
Theo James	—	Kemal Pamuk
Rob James-Collier	—	Thomas Barrow
Allen Leech	—	Tom Branson
Rose Leslie	—	Gwen Dawson
Phyllis Logan	—	Elsie Hughes
Cal Macaninch	—	Henry Lang
Elizabeth McGovern	—	Cora, Countess of Grantham
Sophie McShera	—	Daisy Robinson
Lesley Nicol	—	Beryl Patmore
Amy Nuttall	—	Ethel Parks
Brendan Patricks	—	Evelyn Napier
David Robb	—	Dr Richard Clarkson
Maggie Smith	—	Violet, Dowager Countess of Grantham
Dan Stevens	—	Matthew Crawley
Penelope Wilton	—	Isobel Crawley

FURTHER READING

FAMILY LIFE

Rosina Harrison, Rose: *My Life in Service*, Book Club
Associates, London 1976, with particular reference
to pp20–21, 23.

Juliet Nicolson, *The Perfect Summer*, John Murray,
London 2007, particularly pp15, 151.

Rosina Harrison, *Gentlemen's Gentlemen*, Sphere Books,
London 1978, with particular reference to pp26–7, 31,
44, 46, 77, 167.

Eileen Balderson, *Backstairs Life in a Country House*, David
& Charles, London 1982, particularly pp28–29, 31–32.

SOCIETY

Lady Colin Campbell, *Etiquette of Good Society*, Cassell &
Company, London 1893.

Gail MacColl and Carol Wallace, *To Marry An English Lord:
Or How Anglomania Really Got Started*, Workman,
New York 1989, with particular reference to
pp33, 112, 114–117.

Consuelo Vanderbilt Balson, *The Glitter & The Gold*,
George Mann, Maidstone 1973, particularly p58.

Diana Cooper, *The Rainbow Comes & Goes*, Penguin
Biography, London 1961, particularly pp75–76.

Andrew Marr, *The Making of Modern Britain*, Macmillan,
London 2009, particularly pp148, 149, 302–3.

CHANGE

Andrew Marr, *The Making of Modern Britain*, Macmillan,
London 2009, particularly p70, 86, 89, 38, 41.

Derrik Mercer (editor), *Chronicle of the 20th Century*,
Longman, London 1988.

Max Arthur, *Lost Voices of the Edwardians: 1901–1910
In Their Own Words*, Harper Perennial, London 2007,
particularly p380, 383.

Pamela Horn, *Life Below Stairs in the Twentieth Century*,
Amberley Publishing, Glos 2001, particularly p36.

Juliet Nicolson, *The Perfect Summer*, John Murray, London
2007, with particular reference to 104–6, 99–100.

LIFE IN SERVICE

Rosina Harrison, *Gentlemen's Gentlemen*, Sphere Books,
London 1978, with particular reference to pp106–7, 112,
26, 71, 141, 184, 147–8, 107, 171.

Jeremy Musson, *Up and Down Stairs: The History of the Country
House Servant*, John Murray, London 2008, particularly p7.

Pamela Sambrook, *Keeping Their Place: Domestic Service in
the Country House*, Sutton Publishing Ltd, Glos 2005,
particularly p27 (quoting William Lanceley, 'Hall-Boy
to House Steward', p9), 30, 45.

Juliet Nicolson, *The Perfect Summer*, John Murray,
London 2007, particularly p160.

Rosina Harrison, *Rose: My Life in Service*, Book Club
Associates, London 1976, particularly p36.

Eileen Balderson, *Backstairs Life in a Country House*,
David & Charles, London 1982, particularly p17.

STYLE

Consuelo Vanderbilt Balson, *The Glitter & The Gold*,
George Mann, Maidstone 1973, particularly pp53–4, 93.

Rosina Harrison, *Rose: My Life in Service*, Book Club
Associates, London 1976, particularly pp20–21.

Isabella Beeton, *Mrs Beeton's Houshold Management*,
Wordsworth Reference, 1861.

Lady Colin Campbell, *Etiquette of Good Society*, Cassell &
Company, London 1893.

Juliet Gardiner, *The Edwardian Country House*, Channel 4
Books, London 2002, particularly p127.

Jeremy Musson, *Up and Down Stairs: The History of the
Country House Servant*, John Murray, London 2008,
particularly pp226–7.

Diana Cooper, *The Rainbow Comes & Goes*, Penguin
Biography, London 1961, particularly p107.

Gail MacColl and Carol Wallace, *To Marry An English Lord:
Or How Anglomania Really Got Started*, Workman, New York
1989 – particularly pp68, 70–71.

Ernest King, *The Green Baize Door*, William Kimber,
London 1963, particularly p19.

HOUSE & ESTATE

Pamela Horn, *Life Below Stairs in the Twentieth Century*, Amberley Publishing, Glos. 2001.

Anita Leslie, *Edwardians in Love*, Hutchinson, London 1972.

Juliet Gardiner, *The Edwardian Country House*, Channel 4 Books, London 2002, with particular reference to pp41, 179, 180.

Frances, Countess of Warwick, *Life's Ebb and Flow*, William Morrow & Company, New York 1929, particularly pp108–9, 229.

Anthony J Lambert, *Victorian & Edwardian Country House Life from Old Photographs*, Batsford, London 1981.

Lady Colin Campbell, *Etiquette of Good Society*, Cassell & Company, London 1893.

Diana Cooper, *The Rainbow Comes & Goes*, Penguin Biography, London 1961, particularly pp120–121.

John Lewis-Stempel, *Six Weeks: The Short and Gallant Life of the British Officer*, Weidenfeld & Nicholson, London 2010.

ROMANCE

Frances, Countess of Warwick, *Life's Ebb and Flow*, William Morrow & Company, New York 1929, with particular reference to pp28, 212, 205.

Anita Leslie, *Edwardians In Love*, Hutchinson, London 1972, particularly pp15, 232, 318.

Diana Cooper, *The Rainbow Comes & Goes*, Penguin Biography, London 1961, particularly p67.

Clive Aslet, *The Last Country Houses*, Book Club Associates, 1982, particularly p31.

Rosina Harrison, *Rose: My Life in Service*, Book Club Associates, London 1976, particularly pp23, 24.

Margaret Powell, *Below Stairs*, Pan Books, London 2011, particularly pp116, 189–90.

Andrew Marr, *The Making of Modern Britain*, Macmillan, London 2009, particularly p50.

Richard Holmes, *Tommy: The British Soldier on the Western Front 1914–1919*, Harper Perennial, London 2004, particularly pp483, 597.

Svetlana Palmer and Sarah Wallis, *A War in Words*, Simon & Schuster, London 2003, particularly p227.

Juliet Gardiner, *The Edwardian Country House*, Channel 4 Books, London 2002, particularly p211.

Lyrics to 'The Only Girl in the World' (music by Clifford Grey, Lyrics by Nat D. Ayer), published by kind permission of EMI.

WAR

Vera Brittain, *Testament of Youth*, Fontana/Virago, London 1933/1970, particularly p89, 96, 307, 165, 166–7, 211, 215.

R.H. Tawney, quoted in *The Attack and Other Papers*, Allen & Unwin, 1953.

Brian MacArthur, *For King & Country: Voices from the First World War*, Abacus, London 2009, particularly p12, 75–6, 122–3, 71.

Richard Holmes, *Tommy: The British Soldier on the Western Front 1914–1919*, Harper Perennial, London 2004, particularly p138, 258, 325, 495.

Svetlana Palmer and Sarah Wallis, *A War in Words*, Simon & Schuster, London 2003, particularly pp42–3, 188–9.

John Lewis-Stempel, *Six Weeks: The Short and Gallant Life of the British Officer*, Weidenfeld & Nicholson, London 2010, particularly p122, 125–6, 60, 160.

Richard Holmes, *Shots From the Front*, Harper Press, London 2010, particularly p127.

Geoff Bridger, *The Great War Handbook*, Pen & Sword Books, South Yorkshire 2009, particularly p107, 113, 139.

Rosina Harrison, *Gentlemen's Gentlemen*, Sphere Books, London 1978, particularly p161.

Andrew Marr, *The Making of Modern Britain*, Macmillan, London 2009, particularly p151.

Derrik Mercer (editor), *Chronicle of the 20th Century*, Longman, London 1988.

Norman Lowe, *Modern British History*, Palgrave Macmillan, Hampshire 2009, particularly p448.

ALSO

Nicholas Bentley, *Edwardian Album*, Sphere Books 1981.

Mary Borden, *The Forbidden Zone*, Hesperus Press Limited, London 2008.

Mark Girouard, *Life in the English Country House*, Penguin Books, London 1980.

Eilnor Glyn, *Three Weeks*, Digit Books (Brown, Watson), London (no date given).

Virginia Nicholson, *Singled Out*, Penguin, London 2007.

Vita Sackville-West, *The Edwardians*, Virago Press, London 1983.

Anna Sproule, *The Social Calendar*, Blandford Press, Dorset 1978.

Who's Who: Titles and Forms of Address, A&C Black, London 2007.

ACKNOWLEDGEMENTS

This book would not have been possible without the original ideas of Gareth Neame and Julian Fellowes and I am entirely grateful for their enormous generosity in allowing me to write about their created world. Thanks, too, to Carnival Films, chiefly David O'Donoghue, and the series producer Liz Trubridge, for their patient help and encouragement in making this book happen. The exceptional talent of the Downton Abbey crew have also contributed to this book – whether indirectly through their telling of the story on the screen or directly because they generously gave their time, explaining to me how it all happened, particularly Donal Woods, Judy Farr, Corina Burrough, Mark Kebby, Susannah Buxton, Rosalind Ebbutt, Anne 'Nosh' Oldham, Phillippa Broadhurst and Lucy Spofforth.

Thank you to everyone at HarperCollins and their extraordinary dedication to producing the most beautiful book they could, particularly Helen Hawksfield, picture researcher Sally Cole and designer Myfanwy Vernon-Hunt. Thanks, too, to Louise Stanley for her kind and clever editing and Publisher Hannah MacDonald for her faith in me.

Thanks to Victoria Brooks and Una Maguire of Milk Publicity for all their good-humoured help. Thank you to my agent Rowan Lawton and her colleague Annabel Merullo at PFD, who made it all happen in the first place.

I would like to make special mention of the authoritative voices, research and astute remarks of Adam Jacot de Boinod, Jeremy Musson, Anne de Courcy and Emma Kitchener-Fellowes. Thank you. This book would not have been possible without the scholarship of many better authors than I, particularly Juliet Nicolson, Gail MacColl, Carol Wallace and Andrew Marr. I also hope this book brings to life again the wonderful voices of Rosina Harrison and her 'gentlemen's gentlemen', Daisy Warwick, Diana Cooper and Consuelo Vanderbilt. They deserve to be heard.

And finally but far from last – thank you to my family: Simon, Beatrix, Louis, George and Cordelia. Without you, I couldn't have done it at all.

Printed and bound in U.S.A. by
R R Donnelley

www.stmartins.com

Downton Abbey
A Carnival Films/Masterpiece Co-Production

Library of Congress Cataloging-in-Publication Data Available Upon Request

ISBN 978-1-250-00634-9

Originally published in the United Kingdom by Collins,
an imprint of HarperCollins*Publishers*

First U.S. Edition: December 2011

3 5 7 9 10 8 6 4 2